The Accountant Beside You
presents

Church Accounting

The How -To Guide for Small &
Growing Churches

Books by Lisa London

The Accountant Beside You series

QuickBooks® for Churches and Other Religious Organizations

Using QuickBooks® for Nonprofit Organizations, Associations & Clubs

QuickBooks® para Iglesias y Otras Organizaciones Religiosas

The Accountant Beside You

presents

Church Accounting

The How-To Guide for Small & Growing Churches

Lisa London, CPA

with

Vickey Boatright

Deep River Press, Inc.
Sanford, North Carolina

The Accountant Beside You presents

Church Accounting—The How-To Guide for Small & Growing Churches

ISBN 978-0-9911635-3-3

Library of Congress Control Number 2014918338

Published by Deep River Press, Inc. November 2014

EDITED BY Susan Sipal

OVER DESIGN BY Greg Schultz and Shannon Parrish

Dedicated to the memory of my precious husband, Kevin Boatright, who never stopped believing in me.

Vickey Boatright

Table of Contents

Acknowledgements

I would like to thank Terressa Pierce of Freechurchforms.com for her wisdom and contributions to the book.

Once again, Susan Sipal was my editor extraordinaire, helping me not sound too much like an accountant.

And special thanks to my godfather, Vince Miller, CPA for his help, support, and mentoring. He is a man I will always look up to.

Lisa London

Introduction

Welcome to *Church Accounting—The How-To Guide for Small and Growing Churches*. I'm Lisa London, a CPA with decades (I hate to admit how many) of experience helping churches, nonprofits, and businesses of various sizes with their accounting systems, and I'm here to guide you through this important but often frustrating process.

After writing *QuickBooks for Churches and Other Religious Organizations*, I realized the strong need for a resource to help small and growing churches set up their offices and accounting systems in a cost-effective manner. You can't research anything about church accounting on the web without ending up at Vickey Boatright's site, www.freechurchaccounting.com, so I enlisted her help to put together this step-by-step guide to accounting for churches.

Vickey worked as a fund accountant for a nonprofit for over 12 years and is a staff accountant for Wisdom Over Wealth, an accounting firm in Massachusetts. Her site, www.freechurchaccounting.com, averages 30,000 visitors a month and is a treasure trove of valuable information on all things churches! Started in 2008, her site has grown exponentially with information on all of the ins and outs of church accounting. Besides the website, with her late husband's encouragement, she started and also maintains www.basicaccountinghelp.com for small business owners. She is the treasurer for her church of 37 years and, in spite of all of her activities, still has time to play with her six grandchildren.

Together, we'll guide you through the processes, procedures, and steps for your church to have an efficient and effective accounting system. Accounting for churches is different. We will do our best to explain it in a way you don't need an accounting degree to understand. Then we'll get into the meat of the matter. You will learn how to handle different types of contributions, including designated funds or grants.

Bill paying can get complicated when there are expenses to allocate across programs, credit card statements, and petty cash. Reimbursements will also be covered.

Payroll is a crucial part of any organization, and rules for pastors are very different than normal payroll. Pastors are also entitled to special tax treatment for housing that will be reviewed.

Instrumental to achieving your church's mission is having a clear view of your church's financial health. We will step you through the planning stages with budgets and the reporting and forecasting needs.

Vickey and I have designed spreadsheets, letters, resolutions, etc. which we share throughout the book. As a convenience, we offer these for sale as a package on www.accountantbesideyou.com. If time is of a concern, this easy download may be cost-effective but, if you prefer, the information is here in the book to do it yourself.

I know this is a lot to cover, but remember, as **The Accountant Beside You**, I am with you all the way!

Lisa London

I.   Proper Procedures and Internal Accounting Controls

Churches are fortunate to enjoy special privileges in regards to tax laws. As with any privilege, there is a cost to protect that benefit by being extra careful with the accounting and internal controls. This can seem difficult for small churches who rely on volunteer labor or overworked pastors.

Pastors are typically good people who are very caring with strong interpersonal skills. These skills do not necessarily translate to understanding accounting rules, tax laws, and internal accounting controls. The lack of understanding can lead to the loss of donors' tax benefits, monetary penalties for the church, and even prison time.

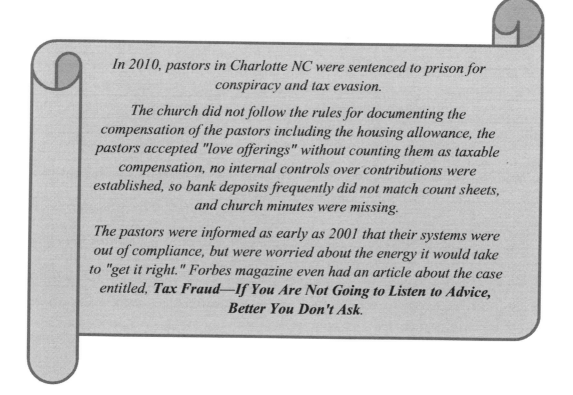

In 2010, pastors in Charlotte NC were sentenced to prison for conspiracy and tax evasion.

The church did not follow the rules for documenting the compensation of the pastors including the housing allowance, the pastors accepted "love offerings" without counting them as taxable compensation, no internal controls over contributions were established, so bank deposits frequently did not match count sheets, and church minutes were missing.

*The pastors were informed as early as 2001 that their systems were out of compliance, but were worried about the energy it would take to "get it right." Forbes magazine even had an article about the case entitled, **Tax Fraud—If You Are Not Going to Listen to Advice, Better You Don't Ask**.*

In the previous example, the church had to file for bankruptcy to avoid a foreclosure sale as the succeeding pastor and the congregation struggled to keep the church alive. As with any case, there is more to the story than can be summarized here, but the lesson to be learned is:

> *Strong, appropriate accounting processes and controls are required for a church to be a good steward of its gifts.*

In this chapter, we'll review:

- The need for strong internal controls.

- The governing body's responsibilities.

- How to deal with separation of duties with a small staff.

- Detailed procedures for handling the money coming in and leaving the church.

A.   The Need for Strong Internal Controls

With my experience as an auditor of businesses and nonprofits, I saw first-hand what a difference strong internal controls can make to an organization. People often think of internal controls only as a means to keep employees from stealing. And many people assume that if someone works for a church, they would never steal.

In case you think likewise, do an Internet search on "stealing money from a church." The over 12 million results should disavow you of that notion. People are human and money does get stolen from churches, even by the pastors. Setting up proper controls will help stem that possibility.

Internal controls are not only in place to protect against fraud, but to keep errors from occurring or to make it easier to catch when they do. A good bookkeeper will require strong internal controls to keep themselves above suspicion. Additionally, *you* know that you wouldn't steal from the church, but having controls in place gives you reassurance that the person who takes over after you are gone will also not steal.

The smaller the organization, the harder it is to have separate people in the required positions to maintain strong controls. But don't worry, this book will highlight options and ideas to put in place to make this work for your situation.

The most basic start for establishing internal controls begins at the governing body level (whether a vestry, council, or board). A strong governing body with transparency, stewardship, and accountability sets the tone and is the first defense against fraud.

B.   Governing Body's Responsibility

The governing body has a very important role to play in setting the tone for financial management. Besides serving as counsel for the pastor and offering direction for the church's mission and goals, the members of the governing body are responsible for the assets of the church. In order to maintain good stewardship, I recommend the following:

- Financial statements should be reviewed by council on a regular basis (monthly or quarterly).
- Annual budgets should be prepared and variances reported on a regular basis.
- There should be a designated treasurer who is NOT the bookkeeper.
- Any notices from the IRS must be given unopened to someone who is NOT the bookkeeper. *
- A conflict of interest policy needs to be established. (This does not mean church or council members can't do business with the church. It simply limits the level of related party transactions and determines steps to make certain the most appropriate price is paid.)
- An annual audit must be performed. If the church cannot afford an outside auditor, designate an audit committee composed of members not associated with the accounting part of the church.

* A far-too-common occurrence is for the bookkeeper to steal the federal or state withholding from employees' payroll and not pay the IRS. If the same bookkeeper receives the notices from the IRS, he can stall the discovery of the fraud for years.

Next, I will outline specific controls to use for each area of the accounting system. As you read through these, keep in mind this basic rule:

> *The person with access to the records MUST NOT have access to the funds!*

This means the person entering the data in the accounting system or tracking donor contributions should not have access to the checking account or plate collections. I realize this may seem counter-intuitive. But think through why I have told you this basic rule.

If a donor hands me (as the bookkeeper) a check to be deposited, I can deposit the check into a dummy account that I control and then send a donor acknowledgement from the church to the donor. The donor assumes the church has received it as they have written confirmation, and the church never knew they were supposed to get it, so they do not know it is missing. If, however, the check was given to a separate person to deposit and then a copy of the check or deposit was given to me (as the bookkeeper), I can record the deposit in the financial statements and send out the donor acknowledgement, but I can't touch the money. The person receiving the check could take the money, but the donor would not receive an acknowledgement.

In the accounting world, this is referred to as a "separation of duties." It will not stop all fraud and error, but makes it more likely to be discovered.

In a small church, the treasurer and bookkeeper are often the same person. Sometimes this person is even the pastor. But don't worry. I will give you the tools to implement the necessary controls even with a very limited staff.

C. Separation of Duties with a Small Staff

I can already hear many of you saying, "We are too small to have more than one person helping with the books." I promise you, you are never too small to have the basic controls to protect your staff and assets. The pastor can be the treasurer or the bookkeeper, but not both. If he receives the bills and knows which program should be charged, allow him to enter bills, write checks, and enter donations. But designate someone else from the governing council to sign the checks.

Consider having the people handling the cash for the church bonded. This is an insurance policy against theft. And if you still don't think people steal from churches, check out this website, blog.congregationalsecurityinc.com/tag/embezzlement dedicated to stories of church embezzlements.

If there is a volunteer or part-time assistant in the church office, you can train him to enter the bills and donations and allow the pastor to be the treasurer/check signer.

As long as the pastor has at least one other person he can call on for help, your church can separate the access to the funds from the access to the records.

D. Controls for Receiving Cash & Donations

1. Money Received during Services

If you have regular services, you probably "pass the plate" and ask for donations to keep the church running. The money is passed through the congregation and then brought up to the front of the church in plain sight of all or is taken to a back room to be counted after the service.

The main thing to remember with this collection is the cash should be in sight of two unrelated people (i.e. not husband and wife) until it is counted. There is less likelihood of collusion (two or more people working together to steal) if the counters are unrelated.

Before you repeat the "we don't have enough people" argument, let me offer a few strategies. If at least two unrelated people attend your service, you can ask them to stay for a few minutes to count the money. If you have a council or vestry, you may wish to assign a different council member each week to count with another member of the congregation. This allows for at least one trained person to be counting and also gives the council members the opportunity to see some of the details behind the church.

Once the service is over or once the money has been removed to the backroom, two people should count the cash and checks. Next they need to fill out a summary form showing the amounts and any special donor notations for the cash collection. Each counter will then sign the form. If possible, copies should be made of the checks so any notations or additional information can be seen by the bookkeeper later. A deposit slip should be filled out and copied. The deposit will then be driven to the bank and put in the night deposit. One person can do this as there is a record of the receipts at the church. When the bookkeeper comes to work later that week, he will have the copy of the deposit as a record of what to input into each member's account. Chapter IV will cover this in more detail.

Keep in mind that any restrictions on the donations need to be notated so they can be correctly recorded by the bookkeeper and so appropriate acknowledgements can be sent.

If your church receives a large number of checks, you may wish to ask your bank about an RID—Remote Imaging Device scanner. This allows you to quickly scan the checks and print out a report for your files. The scanned file is automatically sent to the bank, so the deposit can be made immediately rather than waiting on a volunteer to drive to the bank later in the week. Once the bank has the scanned image, it does not need the physical check.

The original checks can be marked with a highlighter to show they were scanned and filed for future reference. The scanner will not let you send the same check twice. Beware though. If you accidentally try to deposit the scanned checks at the bank, a deposit correction fee may be charged.

By scanning the checks immediately after the service, there is less likelihood of someone taking them and depositing them into their own account. The scanner is also less likely to make math errors.

> *Banks usually charge a fee for the RID scanners, but the time savings and control features are often worth the additional expense.*

2. Money Received Through the Mail

Often members or other donors prefer to mail in their donations rather than bringing them to the church. It is a good idea to have a post office box. This keeps anyone from stealing the checks out of your mailbox. You don't want your bookkeeper to be the one to pick up the mail. Theoretically, he could steal some checks but make the member's account look like it was received.

Designate someone without access to the accounting system to go to the post office, and then, back at the church, have him open the mail in front of a second person. Each check should then be recorded and the summary signed by the two observers. If you have an RID scanner, scan the checks immediately, and then give the deposit report and the marked checks to the bookkeeper.

3. Electronic Payments Received Through the Website

Now that so much is being done on the web, many churches have found it advantageous to add a donation button to their website. This can be activated through many different services.

The most important thing to do with electronic payments is to safeguard the link to the bank account. Many online credit card processors will require signed corporate resolutions stating you are a legal organization and the check signers have authorized the funds to go to that account. Others, like PayPal®, simply use an email/password combination. This is potentially a problem as the person who has the password could reroute the appointed deposit bank account to their personal account number.

> *A PayPal employee told me of a women associated with a small nonprofit who had set up its PayPal account. She had a falling out with the organization and refused to tell them the password to collect the money.*

To keep any of these problems from occurring with your church, I would recommend the account be linked to an email address administered by your church (admin@yourchurch.org) and assigned to someone who has no access to the members' records. This person would have the authorization to change the bank deposit account number and permit transfers from the PayPal account to the bank. As they could change the bank account number to their personal account, they should NOT have access to the member records.

PayPal does allow for a secondary user with limited rights that can only see reports, not change bank account numbers. This person can verify the amounts received in PayPal were recorded in the church's accounting records. You will want this to be your bookkeeper so he can reconcile the receipts PayPal is reporting to the cash posted into the bank. Any discrepancies should be investigated immediately.

E.   Donor Acknowledgements

One way to assure the same amount of money donors have given has been recorded in your accounting records is to send donor acknowledgement forms on a regular basis. At a minimum, this should be done at year end for the donor's tax purposes, but I recommend doing it quarterly, or at least, semiannually.

Your members probably give money based on their pledge or tithe, some special collections, and perhaps an occasional extra donation to help the church. A donor acknowledgement statement typically gives a summary of all their donations and the amount of pledges still outstanding. It is a powerful tool to thank your donors and also remind them of any outstanding balance.

To use this tool as an accounting control, add a sentence near the bottom for the donor to contact the treasurer or pastor with any questions or differences from the statement. (This assumes the treasurer and pastor are not the bookkeeper.) If you have an office administrator, he should be instructed not to give these calls to the bookkeeper. Any discrepancies between the donor's records and the church's should be investigated by someone besides the bookkeeper. Usually the discrepancies will be recording errors, which can be reviewed with the bookkeeper, but be aware of the possibility of theft.

F.   Fundraisers and Controls

Various groups within the church may need to hold fundraisers to support their activities. People involved in the fundraisers need to be given specific instructions on how to handle any cash received.

If there are raffle or admission tickets, have them printed with numbers and track the ticket numbers by each person selling the tickets. The person should return the unused tickets plus cash equal to the tickets not returned. For example: Mary takes raffle tickets 101-200 with a ticket value of $1 each. Sue logs Mary's name and the ticket numbers she has taken. At the end of the event, Mary turns in ticket stubs for ticket numbers 101-125 with the purchasers name and $25. She also turns in tickets numbered 126-200. Sue logs the numbers sold and the numbers returned for Mary and all sellers.

With another person present, Sue counts the money at the end of the event, compares it to the log of money received, investigates any differences, signs it acknowledging the amount, and deposits the money in the bank. The log and deposit slip are left at the church for the bookkeeper to record.

If a carnival style fundraiser is being held, consider selling food/game tickets at one booth to be used throughout the carnival. This keeps the volunteers at each booth from having to handle and track cash. The booth receiving cash should always have two unrelated people and have pre-numbered tickets.

For other types of fundraisers, ask yourself, "What is the best way to be certain the money donated is deposited in the church account?" The procedures and controls can be designed around the answer to that question.

We've covered some basic steps to protect your people and your money in the most common ways donations are received. Now make a list of all the other ways money is received and ask yourself—for each case, how you can get it to the bank and recorded in the financial statements while providing good stewardship of your gifts and protecting your volunteers and employees?

> *These are the minimum steps to take to safeguard cash. If your church already has more complete procedures, please follow them.*

G.   Cash Out—Controls for Paying Bills & Credit Cards

Fraud, theft, and mistakes are as much of a concern with the money going out as they are with the money coming in. Procedures and controls need to be in place to keep phantom employees or fake vendor invoices from being paid. To assure good stewardship over your church's money, you will need strong accounting controls in place as it relates to the money paid out. The next few sections will cover some basics for the outgoing controls.

> *Remember the basic rule. If someone has access to the money, he should not have access to the financial records.*

H.   Check Signers

The bookkeeper must not be an authorized check signer. I know this sounds nearly impossible for a small church, but, here again, you may need to utilize the members of the governing body or other volunteers. No one should ever sign a check made out to himself. If the pastor is a check signer and needs to be reimbursed, the treasurer or other check signer should sign the check.

You need at least two check signers in case one is on vacation or leaves the church. I'd recommend three just to be safe. Stay away from too many signers as a fraudulent bookkeeper could use this to his advantage by submitting the same invoice to be paid twice and pocketing the second payment.

Large purchases should require two signers. The definition of large is determined by the size of your church. If it is common for your church to pay $500 invoices, perhaps the limit should be $1000 for two signers. For the dual signatures to work, the dollar limit must be printed on the check. Keep in mind, however, banks do most things electronically and no longer look for the two signatures.

It is probably a good idea to have printed on your checks, *Not Valid after 90 Days*. This keeps you from having to incur stop payment charges on checks people may have lost.

I. Paying Bills

Bills should not be entered into the system without documentation and approval from someone other than the bookkeeper. This could be the pastor or treasurer. Sometimes the documentation is as simple as the bill from the utility company or a handwritten note asking the supply organist be paid $100. If the expense is to be charged to more than one program, the approver should also notate this. But most importantly, all bills to be paid must be approved. Invoices to be paid should be approved before they are entered into the system and checks cut.

> *The approval process should not be taken lightly. If the pastor or treasurer is not familiar with the vendor, the bill should be questioned. If a large dollar purchase or repair needs to be made, it should be discussed beforehand with the governing body.*

The bookkeeper will enter and code the bills into the correct expense categories and programs or grants. He will then print the checks, match them up with the approved documentation, and give them to an authorized check signer. The check signer should assure himself that the payee, address, and amounts agree to the approved documentation and sign the checks. The invoices should be marked paid to keep from issuing a duplicate check.

I recommend you use a voucher-style check. This is a multi-part check that allows a space for the payee to see what invoice was paid or what the payment was for. A three-part voucher check is also available which allows the bookkeeper to staple the third section to the approved invoice. An example is on the facing page.

The checks can then be mailed and the documentation filed or scanned. I recommend filing by vendor name. Set up a file for each letter of the alphabet and place infrequently paid vendors invoice in its appropriate file. Saving them as electronic scans is fine as long as the related check number is notated and the scans are adequately backed up offsite. Also, set up a naming and filing protocol for scanned files for ease of retrieving the data.

J.   Automatic Drafts

Automatic drafts for recurring bills can be a convenient feature for a church. They are often used to pay the payroll processor or utility bills. However, it is just as important to review them for reasonableness as it is for any other bill.

Most vendors send an email or mail a bill stating the date and amount of the automatic draft. These should be reviewed and approval noted by the treasurer then held in a pending file until the bank account is reconciled.

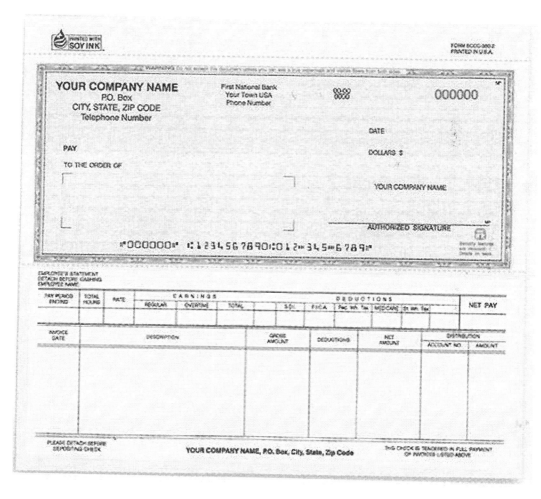

K.   Petty Cash

Often volunteers or employees of the church may need to make a quick run for supplies or other small dollar items. If the bookkeeper and check signers are not always available, it may make sense to have a petty cash fund.

This is often called an *imprest* fund, which means the fixed fund is only replenished after the money is spent. Assuming a church has a petty cash fund of $100, cash can be given to a person to buy supplies. If $20.00 is given, the person is required to bring back a receipt for the amount spent and any change from the $20.00. At the end of the month, the drawer or envelope holding the petty cash should have receipts and cash totaling $100. The receipts are then used as support for the replenishment check.

For example, Your Church has $100 in their petty cash fund. Throughout the month, various volunteers used the money and brought back the following receipts:

> $9.95 for donuts for the youth group meeting
> $44.37 for gas to take members to the Habitat for Humanity house
> $15.68 for copier paper for the office

The receipts total $70.00. There should be $30.00 of cash also in the drawer. A check for $70.00 should be made out to Your Church (never Cash, as the check is for the church, not whoever is cashing it) with the receipts as the support for the check signer to review. The check can then be cashed and the drawer replenished. Here is an example using a simple spreadsheet.

	Your Church Petty Cash				
Date	Person Requesting Funds	Purpose	Program	$ Out	$ In
01-Jun		To Start Fund			100.00
05-Jun	Mary Smith	Donuts	Youth Group	9.95	
15-Jun	Jack Rios	Gas for Habitat trip	Outreach	44.37	
29-Jun	Liza Jenkins	Copier Paper	Admin	15.68	
	Total			$ 70.00	$ 100.00
	Balance				$ 30.00

The person responsible for the petty cash fund should be the one in the church office the most. The monthly count needs to be performed by someone else.

L.   Gift Cards or Prepaid Store Cards

Some churches may find it easier to use prepaid store cards or gift cards instead of a petty cash fund. If so, the same basic procedures should be followed. A log of persons holding the gifts cards and the amounts must be maintained. Those persons must be able to show at any time that the receipts plus the balance of the card equal the purchase price of the card.

M. Credit Cards

If your church uses a credit card, appropriate procedures need to be documented so volunteers and employees understand how and when the card can be used. Once you have determined who can use the card and when it is appropriate, you'll need to decide how often you would like the receipts brought in.

Some bookkeepers prefer the receipts be brought to them as soon as possible so cash requirements can be monitored. Others prefer to have the user fill out a form once a month before the bill is due with all of the receipts attached. Either way, the receipts need to be approved by an appropriate reviewer before the credit card bill is paid. Personal expenses should not be allowed to be charged to the church's card. Any personal charges that were inadvertently charged to the card should be repaid immediately.

	Your Church Credit Card Receipts			
Your Name		Approved by.		
Month				
Date	**Vendor**	**Purpose**	**Program**	**Amount**
06/05/2014	Kinkos	Copies for service	Worship	$ 64.95
06/08/2014	Exxon	Gas for Van	Youth	48.68
Total *				113.63
* must agree to credit card bill				

Receipts are attached before bill is approved and paid.

N. Other Payment Controls to Consider

Another way money can be stolen from a church is to issue payments for legitimate bills twice and then deposit the extra check into a dummy account. This often occurs when there are several check signers. One way to guard against this is for the treasurer to review the returned checks from the bank to see if they were endorsed properly and not duplicated. Additionally, the treasurer will need to review the check register on a regular basis looking for duplicate payments or unknown vendors.

In summary, any money leaving the church needs to be approved by someone other than the person requesting the money.

O.   Payroll

For many churches, payroll is the largest expense. Payroll can be processed through an outside service, by the bookkeeper, or by a combination of the two. Regardless of the way it is paid, the church must maintain some basic records which will be discussed in Chapter 7.

The best control for payroll is to require employees to use direct deposit. This assures the check goes directly to the employee's bank account and cannot be taken before they have a chance to get to the bank.

If timesheets are used, they must be approved by the employee's manager and given to the bookkeeper. The bookkeeper should prepare the payroll and review it with the pastor or treasurer before submitting to the payroll service or cutting the checks. Every employee should be known by the person approving unless you have a very large church.

If a payroll service is used, the pastor or treasurer should be the point person to authorize additions of new employees, not the bookkeeper.

The treasurer or pastor must also be certain that all withholding and taxes are submitted to the government. Look for electronic payments or checks monthly or quarterly. Ask your accountant or payroll provider for the rules for your specific church. Any letters received from the IRS must be given unopened to the treasurer or pastor, NOT the bookkeeper. Not paying withholding is a very common way to steal money from an organization.

P.   Summary

Strong internal controls are necessary to keep the church's assets, employees, and volunteers safe. Remember, no organization is too small for strong controls. You now have a blueprint to design the procedures and controls for your church.

We've reviewed the controls needed for churches of all sizes. Next, let me explain how the accounting works in a church environment.

II.   What is Special About Accounting for Churches?

You may have some experience with bookkeeping or accounting for a business or your personal finances and are wondering, how can church accounting be any different?

The big difference is that a church is not concerned with net income or how much money it made. Instead, your church must be certain the money it raised was spent as the donors intended.

A church will receive donations for many different areas; general support of the church, an outreach program, a capital campaign, or maybe an endowment. Some of the money given, like the Sunday offering, is considered unrestricted. It is assumed the church will use this money as needed, and the donor has not requested any particular use of the funds.

Other times, money will be received for a very specific purpose—an outreach program or a capital campaign, or for a specific time—say next year's pledge. Then the money is considered temporarily restricted. This means it can only be used for the purpose or time period the donor has specified. When the restriction is met, i.e. the building is built or a new year has begun, then it becomes an unrestricted asset. If land is donated for the construction of a new church or an endowment is started that only the investment earnings may be spent, a permanently restricted fund must be set up.

In this chapter, I'll explain:

- Accounting terms and processes.
- The difference between cash and accrual basis of accounting.
- What a chart of accounts is and how to design one.
- The basic steps in bookkeeping.
- How church accounting is different from business accounting. This will give you the background you need to handle your church's basic bookkeeping.

A.   Accountant's Speak—Modified Fund Accounting

When speaking with an accountant, you often hear terms like FASB and GAAP as they explain the need to track something a certain way. FASB stands for the Financial Accounting Standards Board and GAAP is the Generally Accepted Accounting Principles that stem from the FASB rules.

Nonprofit organizations' reporting is governed by SFAS (Statement of Financial Accounting Standards) Numbers 95, 116, 117, and 124 which describe how they should account for contributions, present their financial statements, and account for certain investments. You don't actually need to remember these specifically, but you can nod your head intelligently when your accountant mentions one of these alien terms to you.

Also, as most churches do not need to report to outside agencies, they do not have to follow all of the specifics of various SFAS. If you are required to have an outside audit by a donor, bank, or other organization, you will need to work with your outside accountants to determine how to make your financial statements GAAP compliant.

In this book, we will focus on designing the accounting system to give the church management the clear information they need to support the mission of the church and be good stewards of its assets. The system will not be completely GAAP compliant, but close enough that the church's auditors can make the appropriate adjustments if GAAP financials are required.

What you need to know regarding GAAP and SFAS is that, in accounting jargon, as a nonprofit organization, churches are required to keep their accounting records using a modified form of *fund accounting*. A *fund* is defined as a discrete accounting entity with its own set of accounts that must balance the cash and other assets against the liabilities and reserves of the organization. That is a wordy way of saying each significant donation (funds given for a particular purposes) should be tracked separately. But as most churches don't keep separate bank accounts for each fund, you will be using a bit easier system called net assets to track your funds.

*A fund is **NOT** an asset account. It is not a checking or savings account.*

For reporting purposes, these funds can be combined by the restrictions placed on them and tracked by net assets. Net assets are the components of equity in the church. It is what is left over after the liabilities (what is owed) are subtracted from the assets (what the church owns). In the business world, this would be the accumulated profit or loss of the company and is called *retained earnings*.

Net assets are divided into three categories:

- Total Unrestricted Net Assets,
- Total Temporarily Restricted Net Assets,
- Total Permanently Restricted Net Assets.

Unrestricted net assets are donations given to the church to be used for any purpose. Your plate and pledge donations are usually unrestricted and go first toward the operating expenses of the organization.

Temporarily restricted net assets are restricted by the donor based on purpose or time, but the restrictions are not permanent. An example of a *purpose restriction* is when money is given to support the building of a new community center. The money cannot be used for anything but the costs to build the building. If the building is not built, the donor must be contacted to see if the money must be returned or if the donor will authorize its use for another project. As the building is built, the restriction is released, so the money can be given to the vendors.

> *You are not required to open a separate bank account for each restricted fund, but in your accounting records, all expenses and future donations are accounted for in the restricted fund general ledger.*

The other type of temporarily restricted net assets is the *time restriction*. An example of this may be money given in this year to support the church the following year. Prepaid pledges at the end of the year are considered a temporarily restricted net asset.

Permanently restricted net assets are restricted by a donor for a designated purpose that will never expire. These are usually an endowment where the income is used for operations or a program, but the principal must be kept intact.

I have seen some churches with just two or three funds, and I've seen some with 20 or more. The more funds you have, the harder it is on your volunteers or staff trying to keep up with them all. Try to combine as many as you can; however, if the project or program has its own income coming in and expenses going out—**set it up as a fund**.

Which Type of Fund?	Unrestricted	Temporarily Restricted	Permanently Restricted
Plate Offerings or Regular Donations	X		
Pledges for This Year	X		
Pledges for Next Year		X	
Donations for a Youth Trip		X	
Money Towards the New Building Fund		X	
Endowments		X	X

Let me stop here and explain that some nonprofit and church treasurers or finance administrators may think you need to open a separate checking account for each fund. This approach requires a lot more paperwork. It also makes it more difficult on your volunteers and staff to keep the books accurate.

I am not saying you can't open multiple bank accounts. Having a specific bank account for a restricted fund such as building can be beneficial. Evaluate whether the extra effort is worth the benefit of opening the account.

The three most important reasons for a nonprofit to use fund accounting methods are:

1. With fund accounting, *accountability* is measured instead of profitability.

2. Financial reports are directed toward contributors, church members, or the nonprofit's governing body, who are more concerned with having

adequate fund balances to carry on services provided rather than seeking a profit on investments as investors do.

3. In fund accounting, *funds* are set up to provide reporting of expenditures for *designated purposes*.

You should set up and use an accounting system that can detail expenditures and revenues for multiple funds. Each fund should have its own *general ledger*. **The general ledger is the complete record of the financial transactions for a fund or organization and often referred to as the GL.** You would then be able to produce reports that detail each fund's individual income and expenses as well as summarize and total all of the organization's funds.

B. Accounting 101

We have gone over how church accounting is different than business accounting, but now it is time to cover how to do basic accounting. If you are already familiar with debits, credits, assets, and liabilities, go ahead and skip to the next chapter. If not, I'll try to walk you through as painlessly as possible.

Assets are things the church owns or is owed. This includes the bank and investment accounts, pledges receivable, buildings, furniture, and equipment. It can also include expenses you've paid for but not yet used, like prepaid insurance or prepaid postage.

Liabilities are what the church owes. The mortgage to the bank, the credit card bill, payroll due to employees, and payroll taxes due to the government are all liabilities.

Net assets are what are left. They are separated into unrestricted, temporarily restricted, or permanently restricted as we discussed previously.

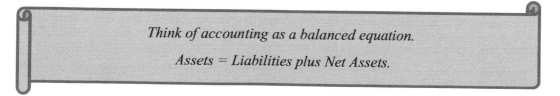

Think of accounting as a balanced equation.

Assets = Liabilities plus Net Assets.

Additionally, you will have income and expenses. Poppy Davis, CPA, sums up the accounting terms wonderfully in her *Small Nonprofits QuickBooks Primer*. I've changed the wording slightly to relate more to churches.

Assets stick around—Expenses go away. If you buy a stove, it sticks around, so it is an asset. If you hire a repairman to fix the stove, he goes away, so the repair cost is an expense.

Income is yours—Liabilities belong to others. If you receive a donation to feed others, it is income, but if you borrow money from the bank to build a new kitchen, it is a liability.

Net Assets are what are left over for your church.

C.   Cash vs. Accrual Accounting Methods

I'm afraid I need to throw a little accounting terminology at you before we go on. There are two methods to track expenses and revenues in the accounting world—Cash and Accrual. The *cash method* is the simplest. The cash is recorded in the financial statements when it is physically received and when the checks are written. The *accrual method* requires dating the transaction when the income was earned (i.e. when the grant was awarded) or the expense item was ordered, not when cash changed hands or the check was written.

For businesses or organizations that pay taxes or are publically held, the difference is significant. Churches can use either depending on their governing boards and other requirements. Assume you receive an invoice from a contractor who did repairs on the church dated July 31, but you didn't write him a check until August 15. If you are using the accrual method, enter the invoice with a date of July 31. Your financial reports for July would show the expense and its offset in accounts payable. If you wanted your reports to reflect the cash method, you would record the expense when it was paid in August.

Most smaller churches use the cash method or a modified cash method, which reflects current amounts due to vendors.

*The **accrual method** gives you the most accurate financial picture of your church; showing money you have earned and expenses you have incurred. The **cash basis** gives you a better idea of when the money has come in or gone out.*

D.   Chart of Accounts

In order to keep track of the assets, liabilities, income, and expenses, we use accounts. The list of all accounts is called the *Chart of Accounts*. I am a firm believer is using a very simple chart of accounts and then tracking things by programs.

Depending on the accounting system you are using, you will want to group similar accounts together using account numbers, as shown below. Notice the Ask My Accountant account. This is a placeholder to record transactions when you are not sure where they should go. It should be cleared out each month once you've verified the correct location with your accountant.

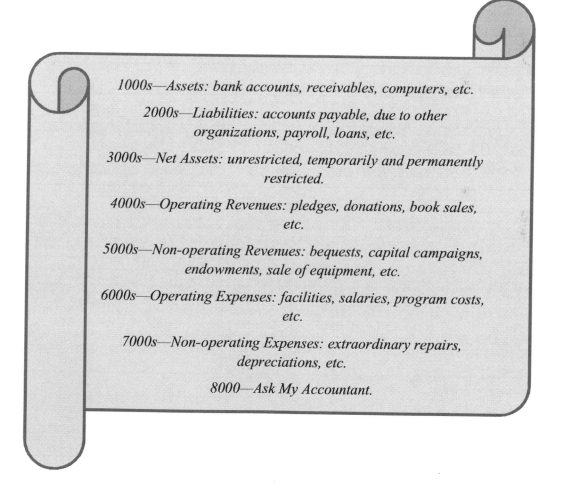

1000s—Assets: bank accounts, receivables, computers, etc.

2000s—Liabilities: accounts payable, due to other organizations, payroll, loans, etc.

3000s—Net Assets: unrestricted, temporarily and permanently restricted.

4000s—Operating Revenues: pledges, donations, book sales, etc.

5000s—Non-operating Revenues: bequests, capital campaigns, endowments, sale of equipment, etc.

6000s—Operating Expenses: facilities, salaries, program costs, etc.

7000s—Non-operating Expenses: extraordinary repairs, depreciations, etc.

8000—Ask My Accountant.

Within this structure, I recommend using the following for the balance sheet asset accounts:

1101-1299	Cash and investments,
1301-1399	Receivables—amounts owed to you,
1401-1499	Prepaid assets—this can be insurance, postage, etc.,
1501-1699	Available for current assets categories in the future,
1701-1799	Church buildings, real estate, and equipment and the related depreciation,
1801-1899	Available for long-term assets categories in the future,
1901-1999	Other long-term assets.

As you can see, this chart gives you 99 accounts under each of the categories. There is an example chart of accounts in Appendix A. It is the one I designed for *QuickBooks for Churches and Other Religious Organizations* and uses this numbering scheme for the liability, equity, revenue, and expense accounts.

> *A **current asset** or **liability** is due or used within a year. A **long-term asset** or **liability** is available or due in more than a year. For example, a pledge made for the next year is a current asset, but a capital campaign contribution due in five years is a long-term asset.*

Within these ranges, you may also have sub-ranges, especially in the expense categories. For example, the facility costs may be in 6000-6399, personnel expenses in 6400-6599, and program expenses from 6600-6999. As you need to add accounts within a range, consider adding them by 10s so you will have space between accounts. With Worship Program Expenses at 6610 and Youth Program Expenses at 6620, you have 10 accounts to add between those two.

E. Naming the Accounts

Now that you have figured out your numbering system, you need to determine how you are going to name the accounts. This sounds very basic, but if you aren't careful, you may have accounts called "Postage and Mailing," "Postage," "Post," etc., which should all be combined. In order to keep things simple, have a policy that significant words are written out with no punctuation marks, and ampersands (&) are used instead of the word "and." If you already have a naming protocol, by all means use it.

F.   Basic Bookkeeping

In the beginning, a church may start out with a simple checkbook and a spreadsheet showing where the money came from and where it is going to.

								Revenues		Expenses
				Cash In	Cash Out	Balance	Donations	Mission	Postage
DATE	Check/Deposit #	Payee/Payor	Purpose						
01-Jun	1	Joe Wilson	donation	200.00		200.00	200.00		
04-Jun	101	USPS	Roll of Stamps		37.00	163.00			37
04-Jun	2	Mary Smith	gift	100.00		263.00	100.00		
						263.00			
						263.00			
						263.00			
						263.00			
						263.00			
						263.00			
Total				$ 300.00	$ 37.00		$ 300.00	$ -	$ 37.00

This is an adequate way to keep track of the money coming in and going out as long as there are very few transactions. Once you start to issue more checks and have more donations brought in for specific things, you will want to have a *double-entry accounting system.*

Let me explain double-entry to you. This simply means every transaction has two sides. Accountants refer to these sides as *debits* and *credits*. They are not good or bad; they are simply opposite sides of an equation.

The check register example above uses a double-entry even if you didn't realize it. Cash deposited from a donation increased the cash (debited) and increased the revenues (credited) by the same amount. The roll of stamps decreased cash (credited) and increased expenses (debited) by the same amount.

Debits and credits affect each type of account, assets, liabilities, equity, income, and expense in a particular way.

Impact of Debits & Credits on Account Types		
Account	Debit	Credit
Assets	Increases	Decreases
Liabilities	Decreases	Increases
Equity	Decreases	Increases
Income	Decreases	Increases
Expense	Increases	Decreases

For example, *Cash* is an asset. Any increases to cash will be recorded as a debit and any decreases as a credit. If we receive a donation, we debit cash (because it increased) and need to credit another account, *Revenue.*

Revenue is an income account, and, from the chart above, we see that we need to credit it to increase the income.

If you were to write this out as a journal entry, it would look like this:

	Debit	Credit
Cash	$100.00	
Donations (Revenue)		$100.00

The total amount of the debits **must** equal the credits.

Don't worry if you feel your eyes glazing over at this point. The good news is most accounting programs do the two sides of the entry for you. You rarely have to record actual journal entries. And when you do, know that I will step you through the process.

I know all of this seems crazy, but there is a method to the madness. Bookkeeping is the process of recording monetary transactions in order to prepare useful financial reports reflecting the wellbeing of your organization.

G.   Reporting Differences

Now that you have the basics of what the accounts are, you need to understand how they are pulled together to help make informed decisions. Financial reports are used to compile the individual accounts into summary reports. Financial reports for churches also have different names than those for a business. The *Income Statement* or *Profit & Loss Statement* that tracks income and expenses for businesses is a **Statement of Activities** for churches.

The Statement of Activities allows the governing council to see how much money has been donated and/or received and how the money is being used. Here is a basic example showing the activity of the restricted and unrestricted funds. Note only income and expense accounts are detailed.

Sample Statement of Activity Per Month/Year to Date				
	General Fund	Restricted Funds	Plant Funds	Endowment Funds	Total All Funds
Revenue					
Contributions	309,027	5,472	16,575		331,074
Interest Income	6,132	3,655	640	5,130	15,557
Workshop/Events	733				733
Bequests				10,000	10,000
Total Revenue	**315,892**	**9,127**	**17,215**	**15,130**	**357,364**
Expenses(By Program)					
Worship	98,541	2,435		5,000	105,976
Education	10, 205	750			10,955
Care/Fellowship	9,876	219			10,095
Evangelism	9,545				9,545
Resources	46,723				46,723
Community Relief	3,000	1,934			4,943
Youth	3,025				3,025
Administration	123,786		11,000		134,786
Total Expenses	**304,701**	**5,338**	**11,000**	**5,000**	**326,039**
Increase (decrease) in net assets:	**11,191**	**3,789**	**6,215**	**10,130**	**31,325**
Beg. Net assets	41,730	72,158	446,995	55,370	616,253
End Net assets	52,921	75,947	453,210	65,500	647,578

Assets, liabilities, and equity are tracked by companies in a *Balance Sheet*. A church uses a **Statement of Financial Position** (shown on next page). This report pulls the assets, liabilities, and equity (funds) accounts.

Management can refer to the Statement of Financial Position to see how much cash is in the bank, how much is owed to the church, and how much the church owes to others. It also separates the unrestricted funds from the restricted funds.

For purposes of this book, I'll refer to these reports as Profit & Loss Statement and Balance Sheet as most people are more familiar with these terms. In Chapter 14, we will go over these reports in detail and other required and suggested reports.

Church
Sample Statement of Financial Position
For Month/Year-to-Date

	General Fund	Restricted Fund	Plant Fund	Endowment Fund	Total All Funds
ASSETS					
Cash and Cash Equivalents	62,533	32,947	16,210	8,500	120,190
Account Receivables	1,768				1,768
Pledges Receivables			72,000		72,000
Other Current Assets	4,765				4,765
Land, Buildings, and Equipment			525,000		525,000
Investments	10,000	43,000		62,000	115,000
TOTAL ASSETS	79,066	75,947	613,210	70,500	838,723
LIABILITIES AND FUND BALANCES					
Accounts Payable	3,621			5,000	8,621
Payroll Withholdings	524				524
Deferred Revenue	22,000				22,000
Current Portion Long-Term Debt			10,000		10,000
Long-Term Debt			150,000		150,000
TOTAL LIABILITIES	26,145	-	160,000	5,000	191,145
FUND BALANCES					
Unrestricted	52,921				52,921
Temporarily Restricted		75,947			75,947
Permanently Restricted				65,500	65,500
Net Investments in Plant			453,210		453,210
TOTAL FUND BALANCES	52,921	75,947	453,210	65,500	647,578
TOTAL LIABILITIES AND FUND BALANCES	79,066	75,947	613,210	70,500	838,723

If you are using an accounting program like QuickBooks or Sage, please remember they refer to the people you receive money from as "Customers," so you must remember that Customers = Donors, Parishioners, or Granting Agencies. Grants received will be tracked as "Jobs," and designated monies and programs will be referred to as "Classes." Jobs and classes are ways the accounting software tags information so reports can be run, pulling all the related data together.

H.   Differences in Terminology

Here is a table showing the terminology difference between businesses and church accounting.

Description	Church Terminology	Business Terminology
Your religious organization	Church, Parish, Synagogue, Temple	Company
People or organizations you receive money from	Parishioners, members, donors, etc.	Customers
People you pay money to	Vendors, suppliers, or people you reimburse	Vendors
People who are employed to work at the church	Employees (payroll)	Employees (payroll)
Report to show money in versus money out (track income and expenses)	Statement of Activities	Income Statement or Profit & Loss Statement
Report to show assets (cash, property, etc.) against liabilities (amount owed) to track the accumulated net wealth	Statement of Financial Position	Balance Sheet
Accumulated net wealth/profit	Net Assets	Net Worth
Grants received that need to have the expenses tracked	Grants	Jobs

I. Summary

Accounting for churches requires the use of funds instead of equity accounts. These funds are summarized into net assets based on their restrictions. The donations and expenses are recorded in the general ledger through the chart of accounts. Most smaller churches use the cash basis of accounting which records the transactions when cash is received or spent, not when promised or ordered. Once the transactions are recorded, they are summarized in the Statement of Financial Position (balance sheet) and the Statement of Activities (income statement).

While this book explains the accounting concepts no matter what system you are using, for detailed instructions on how to use QuickBooks in a church environment, I (shamelessly) recommend my book, *QuickBooks® for Churches and Other Religious Organizations,* available at Amazon.com, www.accountantbesideyou.com, and other retailers.

In the next chapter, we'll review how to select an accounting system or develop your own spreadsheet version.

III.   How do I Select an Accounting System?

If you have simply been keeping track of things with a checkbook, it's time to start thinking about how to set up an accounting system to give you the management reports you need. Keeping in mind we need to be good stewards of the gifts given to our church, I recommend looking at any free or low-cost options first. We'll cover some of the more affordable options before analyzing the more expensive, but more robust, commercial programs.

A.   Spreadsheets

Freechurchaccounting.com, Vickey Boatright's top-ranked website, offers a free Excel spreadsheet that can handle a church needing to track only one fund. Vickey has generously designed it for ease of use, and it will give you a basic Profit & Loss statement as well as a comparison to budget report. Freechurchaccounting.com would be the first place to search for complimentary materials that could fulfill your needs.

I've included a couple of screen shots to give you an idea of how the free spreadsheet is laid out. On the next page is a shot of where the data is entered. For detailed instructions on using this worksheet, go to Freechurchaccounting.com and download the spreadsheet. You can easily enter the date, description (who the donation was from or who the check was paid to), the check number, and whether it was an income or an expense.

Account # / Date	Item Description	Ck#	Debit {Expenses}	Credit {Income}	Balance
					0.00

General Ledger
January 2014

Account # / Date	Item Description	Ck#	Debit {Expenses}	Credit {Income}	Balance
1001	Plate Offering / Tithe /				
	Beginning Balance				0.00
					-
					-
					-
					-
					-
	Total		-	-	
1002	Covenant Missions				
	Beginning Balance				-
					-
					-
					-
					-
	Total		-	-	
1003	Marco Missions Support				
	Beginning Balance				-
					-
					-
					-
	Total		-	-	
1004	Presbytery Support				
	Beginning Balance				-
					-
					-
					-
					-
	Total		-	-	
1005	Not Assigned				
	Beginning Balance				-
					-
					-

Once data is entered, a *Profit & Loss Statement* showing the church income and expenses is automatically populated.

January 2014

					Bank 1 - Savings		0
					Bank 1 - Checking		0
	Cash Beginning of Period				Bank 2		0
						$	-

	Revenue Accounts						
	1001	Plate Offering / Tithe /		$	500.00		
	1002	Covenant Missions		$	-		
	1003	Marco Missions Support		$	-		
	1004	Presbytery Support		$	-		
	1005	Not Assigned		$	-		
	1006	External Support / Fundraising & Unkno		$	-		
	1007	Support - Covenant Members		$	-		
	1008	Transfer - into Bank 1 from Bank 2		$	-		
	1009	Transfer - out of Bank 2 to Bank 1		$	-		
	Total Revenue:					$	500.00

	Expenses:						
	2001	Pastor Salary		$	350.00		
	2002	Pastor Housing		$	-		
	2003	Pastor's Ministry & Continuing Educatio		$	-		
	2004	Travel & Travel Allowance		$	-		
	2005	Music & Worship Program & Materials		$	-		
	2006	Christian Education Materials & Supplie		$	-		
	2007	Pulpit Supply		$	-		
	2008	Audio Visual and other Equipment		$	-		
	2009	Ministry Support		$	-		
	2011	Special Events and Projects		$	-		
	2012	Intern Program		$	-		
	2013	Missions & Presbytery		$	-		
	2014	Outside Services, Accounting, Legal, etc		$	-		
	2021	Office Supplies, stationary, postage, mis		$	-		
	2022	Computer costs and supplies		$	-		
	2023	Communications - Internet & Telephone		$	-		
	2024	Unassigned		$	-		
	2031	Janitorial Supplies and Services		$	-		
	2032	Repair and Maintenance - (Non-Covena		$	-		
	2033	Insurance - Liability		$	-		
	2034	Use Agreement (Utilities & Maint. Reser		$	-		
	2035	Unassigned		$	-		
	2041	Food & Beverages		$	-		
	2042	Other Hospitality Related - Incl. Busines		$	-		
	2043	Unassigned		$	-		
	2051	Van Maintenance & Gasoline		$	-		
	2052	Van Insurance		$	-		
	2061	Overdraft Charges		$	-		
	Total Expenses:					$	350.00

| | **Net : Income Gain / (Loss)** | | | | | $ | 150.00 |

| | **Cash End of Period** | | | | | $ | 150.00 |

INTRO / Chart of Accounts / Budget vs. Actual 1 / Summary by Month / GL J

Also available on Vickey's website and on accountantbesideyou.com is a Spreadsheet Package. It is a more complex worksheet which allows for up to five funds. It also includes individual donor worksheets, bank reconciliation worksheets, and much more.

Either of these options is very cost effective and useful for a small or start-up church. But as your church grows and has more restricted funds and more transactions, you will probably want to research more robust, automated accounting programs.

B. Off-The-Shelf Accounting Software

The next price level of options is off-the-shelf software used by businesses. QuickBooks and Sage are two of the most common seen at local office supply stores. They usually run between $200 and $400 and are more than adequate for most church needs. Many people use these programs, so switching bookkeepers does not usually entail a long learning curve. The downside to these programs is that they were designed for businesses, not nonprofits or churches. Specific "tweaking" must be done to record the fund accounting properly, as I have described in my book, *QuickBooks for Churches & Other Religious Organizations.*

C. Church-Specific Accounting Software

There are several large, church-specific programs—ACS Church Accounting and Church Windows are examples. They tend to be rather expensive, but many offer donor management services, volunteer tracking, event management, and all kinds of bells and whistles. If your church can afford an all-inclusive church specific program, you will want to research a variety of options and ask for free demos. Beside the cost, the downside of the church-specific programs includes a longer training period and more complexity.

D. Online Accounting Packages

Several companies are now offering an online accounting option. Vickey recommends Aplos Accounting due to its ease of use and lower cost than other online options. (Go to Freechurchaccounting.com for more information). Web-based accounting packages offer the convenience of getting information without having to go to the church office. They also allow numerous users to see the same information without copying or emailing.

I have three major concerns with online systems: security, reliability of the Internet connection, and ongoing cost. If you decide to use an online program, research their controls against hackers. Remember, a significant amount of confidential data may be included in the financial information.

If you are not completely satisfied with your Internet reliability, using an online program can be very unproductive. If your Internet connection is lost, you can't access your data. Coming from a rural environment, this can sometimes be a significant issue.

Another consideration is the ongoing cost. With a desktop package, once it is paid for, you do not need to spend any more money until you are ready to upgrade. Web-based programs charge a monthly fee for as long as you use the program.

E.   Summary

Here's a table summarizing the options:

Type	Pros	Cons
Spreadsheet	Inexpensive, fairly easy to set up.	Prone to errors, time intensive, limited reporting.
Off the Shelf	Relatively inexpensive, experienced bookkeepers easy to find, easy bank reconciliations, substantial reporting.	Requires careful set up and recording to make fund accounting work, limited donor management options.
Church Specific	Geared towards church management, strong donor database.	Expensive, significant learning curve. Often requires continued licensing fees or technical support fees.
Online	Convenience of working from anywhere, ease of sharing data, automatically upgraded as systems are improved.	Must pay monthly for as long as the system is being used. If the Internet is not working, reports and transactions cannot be accessed. Online data security risks.

One of the ways to determine if you can afford a new program is to understand what your current program is actually costing you.

If you are paying someone $15 per hour to spend 20 hours per month manipulating spreadsheets, that "free" program is costing you $300 per month.

If converting to an automated accounting program will save 5 hours per month, the new program may pay for itself in 5 months.

$300 program /(5 hours x $15 per hour)=5 months

Bottom line, there is no perfect accounting package. You need to evaluate the options based on the following:

- What is your budget?
- What are the ongoing costs (technical support, program updates, monthly fees)?
- How intuitive is the software? Is the learning time significant?
- Is your current computer sufficient for the program?
- Is multi-user capability important?

One of the biggest mistakes you can make selecting an accounting package is to go with the first one you hear about. Research, ask other church bookkeepers, request a demo copy, and play around with the software.

IV. Contributions — Part I: Receiving and Recording

Contributions are the financial life blood of your church. Keeping accurate records of these contributions is imperative for the organization and the donors.

In this chapter, we will cover how to:

- Handle church contributions from the moment they are received until they are recorded in the donor's contribution records and an acknowledgement sent.
- Classify contributions.
- Know what kind of receipts to issue and what details should be included.
- Record noncash contributions and requests for a receipt for donated labor and/or out-of-pocket expenses.
- Understand when or if to issue receipts for gifts and love offerings.
- Accept and acknowledge contributions of automobiles, boats, and airplanes.

A. Internal Controls and Written Policies

In Chapter 1, I explained the need for separation of duties and the necessary controls for receiving cash. Please go back and re-familiarize yourself with these concepts as they are VERY important.

Take the recommendations I made and put them in a written policy for your church. This is for the protection of your volunteers and employees as well as the church. The procedures outlined help guard against mistakes as well as fraud. By having written policies that are shared with your volunteers, it helps to keep everyone above suspicion. There is a handbook available at accountantbesideyou.com to help with the documentation.

The other thing to review with anyone handing the contributions is the importance of confidentiality. Donors may or may not want their contributions publicized. It should be their decision, not some volunteer who happens to see a check and wants to talk about it. Gossiping about the amounts members donate is a sure-fire way to lose donors.

B.   Counting the Weekly Offering

Once you have collected the offerings following the written procedures of your church, the counters need to count the money, record who it came from, and notate any donor restrictions. Vickey designed the sheet on the opposite page to assist the counters. Notice there is an area for both counters to sign, showing their agreement with the total.

You will want your counters to do the following:

- Pay attention to anything written on the memo section of the checks and envelopes received. If a donor notates the money should be used for a particular purpose (flowers or a mission trip), the counters should record it on the summary sheet.
- Examine the date of each check. Some donors may give their check early but not want you to deposit it until their next payday. If a check is post-dated, set it aside in a secure location to be deposited on the appropriate date.
- Be certain the Payee section of the check is filled in. It is safe to assume the church is the intended recipient, but the name of the church needs to be filled in as soon as possible.
- Double check the amount written out is the same amount in the $ blank. If there is a difference, the bank assumes the written out amount is the correct one. Your deposit should reflect the written value. If it is not obvious to the counters that the written amount is the donor's wish, they should contact the donor and ask for clarification.
- Make sure the signature line is signed. Sometimes people are in a hurry and just forget. The bank will most likely send any unsigned checks back, and the church may incur a change in deposit fee. If the check is unsigned, contact the donor to come by and sign it or send a new one.

C.   Example Collection Count Sheet

ABC Church
Collection Count Sheet

Date: _____

☐ Tithes/Offerings ☐ Ministry Event_____

Cash Received: **Bills**   **Qty**   **Amount**   **Total**

                   100.00   _____   _____

                   50.00   _____   _____

                   20.00   _____   _____

                   10.00   _____   _____

                    5.00   _____   _____

                    1.00   _____   _____

          Total Bills Received: $_____

          Total Coin Received: $_____

Checks Received:

Check No.   **Contributor**   **Amount**

_____   _____   _____

_____   _____   _____

_____   _____   _____

_____   _____   _____

_____   _____   _____

_____   _____   _____

_____   _____   _____

_____   _____   _____

_____   _____   _____

_____   _____   _____

_____   _____   _____

_____   _____   _____

_____   _____   _____

_____   _____   _____

_____   _____   _____

_____   _____   _____

_____   _____   _____

        Total Checks: _____

Total Collections: _____

Income from other Ministries included in the deposit:	**Counted By:**
Amount Ministry/Purpose	
_____ _____	1- _____
_____ _____	
_____ _____	2- _____
_____ _____	

D.   Offering Envelopes

Offering envelopes can be a useful tool to remind members to make donations to the church and to assure the money is attributed to the correct donor's account. Each envelope should include:

- The name of the church.
- A place for the donor's full name, address, telephone number, and email.
- A place to indicate possible funds to which the donor may wish to contribute.
- A statement giving the church full control of the funds contributed. I'll explain this next.

IRS Revenue Ruling 62-113 states that the test as to whether or not a contribution is deductible is whether the organization has *full control of the donated funds* and the discretion as to the use.

Full control of the funds does not preclude giving designated gifts. Individuals may restrict their gifts as long as the gift is used for the church's exempt purpose.

An example of the statement is:

ABC Church is a qualified section 501(c)(3) organization. This contribution is donated with the understanding that ABC Church has complete control and administration over the use of the donated funds in order for this contribution to be considered tax deductible under section 170(c)(2).

If envelopes are used, the counters should review each envelope, looking for any restrictions and notes included in the envelope. Any notes found should be attached to the back of the tally sheet for the bookkeeper to review also.

E.   Making the Deposits

After all donations are checked, tallied, and totaled, the counters are ready to deposit the money. It must be deposited intact; meaning cash should not be taken out of it for the reimbursement of a church expense.

All checks must be stamped with a "For Deposit Only" stamp with the church's legal name. The deposits can then be taken to the night drop or, if necessary, locked in a secure location.

If you have an RID scanner (remote imaging device), the checks are scanned, marked with a highlighter to assure they are not scanned twice, and a deposit detail report is printed from the scanner.

The marked, scanned checks are attached to the back of the report along with any notes from the donor and left for the bookkeeper to enter. The cash is tallied and deposited in the bank with a copy of the deposit slip and any notes from the donors for the bookkeeper.

F.   Recording Donor's Contributions

The money has been deposited, but we need to record it in the financial statements and credit the correct donor with the donation. From the tally sheet and/or deposit report, the bookkeeper or administrator can record the donor's contributions. You can use the date the church received the payment, unless the offering comes in near January 1. The IRS has stringent rules regarding year-end donations and receipts. If the church receives a donation in the mail in early January, it should be recorded in the current year, no matter when the check is dated, unless the envelope is postmarked in the previous year.

*If the **postmark** is dated 12/31 or prior, the contribution should be included in the donor's previous year statement; otherwise it is included in the current year regardless of the date on the check.*

Every contribution should be recorded in your donors' records regardless of whether you plan on sending an annual statement to them.

Sometimes it can be difficult to know how to record the contribution to a donor, so we have some general guidelines. These can be modified for your particular church's needs, but are a good starting point.

When recording a check from a joint account:

- If a husband and wife's names are on the check and they both attend your church, record in the husband's name.
- If just the wife attends, record in her name even if the checking account is in her and her husband's name.
- If the wife has her own checking account and uses that account to give contributions, record in her name only unless told differently.
- If there are two unrelated names on the contribution check, record the name of the person who signed the check.

If the contribution check is from a business, it must be recorded as the business's name unless an individual's name appears with the business name.

G.   Credit Card Donations

More churches and nonprofit organizations have websites than ever before. The website is a perfect location to allow members and others to donate money through credit cards or PayPal links. In Chapter 1, we discussed how to set up the controls for online payments. Now we will review how to record the donation and related fees.

When a donor uses a credit card to make a donation, the church is charged a *discount* fee. The discount is the percentage the processor charges the organization for processing the payment. The fee is handled differently based on the processor, but the two main ways it is charged are discussed here.

- The full amount of the donations are added to the churches' checking account, but the discount and service fees are charged against it.

- The donation is discounted by the discount amount, and the net is added to the checking account.

The first scenario is the easiest. Your processor should have a report detailing the persons making donations. You will input the amounts and send them a thank you or acknowledgement as appropriate. Finally, the discount and service fees are entered into your general ledger in the service charge or bank fees expense account.

In the second scenario, the total amount of the donation does not show up in the checking account. Using the processor's reports, you will need to record the total donation under the donor's name and the fees under expenses. The net should be the amount transferred to the checking account.

	Debit	Credit
Donation Revenue		$ 100.00
Checking Account	$ 95.00	
Processing Fee Expense	$ 5.00	

Donor should receive credit for the full amount

Churches encouraging their members to enroll in an automatically recurring donation program have seen a significant increase in the amount of pledges received and the consistency. For example, if Mr. Smith pledges $100 per month but goes out of town for the summer and forgets to send in payments, the church would only receive $900 instead of the expected $1200. Usually, the additional cost of processing the credit card transactions are more than offset by the increased revenue.

H.   Summary

Keep in mind, anytime cash is being handled, two unrelated people should be involved. The person in charge of the donor records should NOT be handling the money. Offering envelopes can be a useful reminder and assist the bookkeeper in recording the donations correctly. You have also learned how to handle credit card donation fees.

Now that you understand how to receive and record cash and credit card donations, let's review the acknowledging and reporting requirements for all donations.

V. Contributions — Part II: Acknowledging

There are very specific IRS rules regarding the tax deductibility of contributions. Additionally, each state has their own laws. As these rules can change, be sure to review tax law changes with your local CPA or tax specialist on an annual basis.

In this section, we will discuss the four primary types of contribution categories and when to issue a contribution acknowledgement. The four categories are Cash, Noncash, Gifts, and Donated Labor and Services. Additionally, we will go over:

- Quid Pro Quo donations
- Reporting requirements for donations of property
- Gifts of vehicles

A. Cash Contributions

Most of your donations will probably be cash and stock (which is treated as cash for these purposes). According to IRS Pub 1771, the donor is responsible for obtaining a written acknowledgement from a charity for any single contribution of $250 or more before the donor can claim a charitable contribution on his/her federal income tax return.

1. Required Information

According to IRS rules, a contributor may only deduct a donation by cash or check if the contributor has a church-issued receipt or bank record of the contribution. The bank record for this requirement includes bank or credit union statements, canceled checks, or credit card statements.

Regardless of the type, the record must show the date paid or posted, the name of the charity, and the amount of the payment.

The church-issued receipt must include:

- Church's name
- Donor's name
- Date of the contribution
- Date the receipt was issued
- Amount of the cash contribution

> *Most importantly, the receipt **must** include a statement indicating:*
>
> *"The donor did not receive goods or services in exchange for their donation other than intangible religious benefits."*
>
> *Unless something WAS received. If so, it is considered a quid pro quo gift. Refer to the quid pro quo section of this chapter for instructions and wording.*

Vickey designed this example of an annual contribution statement. Besides providing a required tax document, a well-written acknowledgement letter also serves as a good donor management tool.

Annual Contribution Statement
Sample

Dear [Donor],

We thank God for you! Your gifts to _____ Church throughout [year] are gratefully acknowledged.

Because of your contributions, our congregation has been able to support the work of Jesus Christ locally, regionally, and around the world. [Briefly mention some examples of what the church was able to do in missions and ministry during the previous year.]

Attached [or "Here" if it is a short list... just list below] is an itemized statement of your contributions for [year], according to our records. If you have any concerns about the accuracy of this information, please let us know.

For income tax purposes, it is important for us to state here that you did not receive any goods or services in return for any of these contributions other than intangible religious benefits. You made these gifts out of your own generosity and commitment to the church.

Once again, thank you for your generous commitment to the work of Jesus Christ through this church.

Sincerely,

Your Name

Church Title

Dated

Note in the example, the donor is being thanked for her support, reminded of the good works her donation funded, and told how much she is appreciated. You want your donor to feel good about herself and your church when she reads this.

> *Do NOT ask for additional money when sending an acknowledgement. This is the time to thank the donor, not to hit them up again.*

2. Timing

At a minimum, annual contribution statements need to be mailed out after the end of the year. These should be received by the donor no later than January 31 in order for your donors to have the tax information they need on a timely basis.

I recommend sending acknowledgements out more frequently. Any large, non-pledged, or tithed gift should be acknowledged promptly (and graciously) upon receipt. This assures the donor the money was received by the church and gives you the opportunity to thank them.

Regular contributions should be acknowledged quarterly or semi-annually. Besides the benefits of communicating with your supporters, this allows another check on your accounting system to assure donations are being received and recorded properly. Don't forget to add a line on the statement letting the donor know who to call if there are any discrepancies. (And this must not be the bookkeeper!)

B. Stock Donations

For the most part, donations of publically traded stock is treated the same as a cash donation. I highly recommend the church have an investment account available for donors to transfer donations of stock. There is a tax benefit to the donor to transfer stock instead of selling the stock and donating cash.

Assume a donor has sold stock valued at $5000 and given the money to the church. If the stock's value has appreciated since the donor acquired it, they must pay taxes on the difference between the sales price and the purchase price. But if he were to transfer the stock to the church instead of selling it, he could deduct the same amount as a charitable contribution but not have to pay the tax on the gain. Instruct your donors to speak to their tax specialist to see if this would be beneficial to them.

C.   Donations Where a Value was Received by the Donor—
Quid Pro Quo

In some situations, a donor may receive more than "intangible religious benefits" with their donation. Perhaps your church held an auction or a dinner to raise money for a program. Anytime something tangible or of monetary value is received by the donor when he makes a contribution, it is considered a *Quid Pro Quo* contribution.

1.   Requirements

Churches are required to provide a receipt for all transactions of $75 or more where a donor makes a payment and receives goods or services in return. The payments are not cumulative; you would only be required to issue a *quid pro quo* receipt for single payments of more than $75.

The receipt must:

- Inform the donor he may only deduct the excess of any money given over the fair market value of goods or services provided by your church. If property was given instead of cash, only the value of the property in excess of the fair market value of goods or services may be deducted.

- Provide the donor with a good faith estimate of the fair market value of the goods or services that the donor received.

- Furnish a disclosure statement in connection with either the solicitation or the receipt of the quid pro quo contribution. The statement must be in writing and must be likely to come to the attention of the donor. For example, a disclosure in small print within a larger document might not meet this requirement. (*ref: IRS Pub 1771: Charitable Contributions*)

In other words, your acknowledgement letter needs to explain to the donor how much of the donation is tax deductible.

> *It is the actual amount paid by the donor that triggers a requirement for a quid pro quo receipt, not the difference between the amount given by the donor and the good faith value of the goods received by the donor.*
>
> *If the donor buys an $80 ticket to a gala with a FMV of $40, an acknowledgement is required, as more than $75 was received by the church.*

2. Example letter

If the church held an event in which a donation was required to attend, your acknowledgement letter may say something like this:

> *"Thank you for your participation in the Mission Trip Night with Chefs. This letter is a formal acknowledgement for federal tax purposes of the gift you made of $_____. You received goods and services in exchange for this gift valued at $_____ (the value of the dinner). Federal tax law permits you to deduct as a charitable contribution only the excess (if any) of your gift over the value of items you received in exchange."*

3. Determining Value

One of the more challenging aspects of a *quid pro quo* donation is determining the value of the good or service received. **The value is calculated by comparing what you would pay for a similar item or service in the same town.** In the example above, if the dinner was semiformal, and a local restaurant would charge $30 for a similar meal, that is the non-deductible amount.

If there is an auction where a member purchased a pie for $50.00 and the local baker sells pies for $10.00, $10 is the non-deductible amount. The donor can deduct the remaining $40.00

The IRS gives the following example on the article: Charitable Contributions - Quid Pro Quo Contributions on their site:

> *For a payment of $1,000, a charity provides an evening tour of a museum conducted by a well-known artist. The artist does not provide tours on a commercial basis. Tours of the museum normally are free to the public. A good faith estimate of the FMV (fair market value) of the evening museum tour is $0 even though the artist conducts it.*

The donor in the above example could deduct the full $1000 because the FMV of the item or serviced received was $0. If tours of the museum were typically $50, only $950 would be considered deductible.

Let's suppose local merchants donated items to your church raffle. Even though the items raffled off were donated and did not cost the church anything, the fair market value would be the cost of the goods if they were bought at full price from those merchants. Your donors could only deduct the difference between the price given to your church and the amount they would have paid at the store.

> *Bottom line:*
> *Do your best to locate the retail or fair market value and make certain the donors are made aware of the amount.*

4. Acknowledgement Possibilities

If you won't be sending formal letters after the event, print up the invitation and/or admission tickets with the required information on it.

The ticket may include a line:

> *Ticket price of $100 for this amazing evening includes a dinner valued at $30. Federal tax law permits you to deduct as a charitable contribution only the excess of your gift over the value of items you received in exchange.*

D. When You Do Not Need Disclosure Statements

We have covered instances in which reports are needed and when acknowledgements are needed for the donors' tax purposes. But there are times that disclosures are not required.

1. Insubstantial or de minimis value

If your church is giving out key chains and tee shirts with the church logo, no disclosure of these gifts is required. These types of things are considered goods or services of insubstantial or *de minimis* value. Examples are the small giveaways a church may offer that are treated as having no value for disclosure purposes, like pencils, church mailings, small Bibles, etc.

The IRS calculates de *minimis* benefits by comparing the fair market value of a benefit received to the amount of the contribution. Currently, if the value of the benefit is not more than the greater of 2% of the contribution or $102, the donor can usually take a full deduction. IRS changes amount for inflation, check IRS.gov for current level. So if you are having a fundraising event and give each donor a photograph of the church with donations of $100 or more, you don't have to worry about disclosures as the photograph's value is less than $102.

2.   Provided Goods or Services at Fair Market Value

Let's look at paid services your church may provide. No acknowledgement is needed when a member of the church receives goods or services at the current market rate. For example, if the church has a preschool, money received for the tuition is not considered a donation but payment for a service, therefore no acknowledgement is due. Likewise, if a check is received for the use of the church for a wedding, even if it is marked by the donor as a "donation," it is not deductible as a service was provided.

Purchases of books, DVDs, hall rentals, etc. are all considered provided goods or services and are not deductible; therefore they should not be included on a contribution acknowledgement.

3.   Provided Intangible Religious Benefits

Intangible religious benefits are how the IRS defines what you receive from the church for your normal offerings. (We may consider the benefits tangible, but we won't be arguing with the IRS about that.)

Per the IRS, intangible religious benefits are benefits provided to contributors by an organization organized exclusively for religious purposes and are not generally sold in commercial transactions. Payments for intangible religious benefits are not *quid pro quo* contributions. In short, we don't have to worry about a fair market value.

An example of an intangible religious benefit is admission to a religious ceremony. The exception also includes *de minimus* tangible benefits, such as wine or wafers, provided in connection with a religious ceremony. The intangible religious benefit exception, however, does not apply to such items as payments for youth camps, tuition for education leading to a recognized degree, travel services, or consumer goods.

Your church is not required to send contribution statements for your regular pledge, tithing, or weekly offering donations. But as we discussed in the previous chapter, contribution statements should be sent as they are a good communication tool with the donor and a strong control tool for the accounting system.

4.   Examples of the *Quid Pro Quo* Rules

Hopefully I haven't confused you too terribly with *de minimis* benefits and *quid pro quo* talk. I'm including some examples of how the *quid pro quo* rules apply to help:

Bake Sales: Payments for items sold at bake sales and bazaars are not usually tax deductible to donors since the purchase price generally equals the fair market value of the item.

Admission to Events: The majority of the time, donors receive a benefit equal to the contribution they gave to attend a church-sponsored event, such as a concert, and no charitable deduction is generated. However, if the contribution is higher than the fair market value, a *quid pro quo* receipt may be required.

Example 1: Your church sponsors a banquet to raise money for a new church sign charging $35 per person. The meal costs the church $10 per person. There is no disclosure requirement since the amount charged was less than $75. However, the amount deductible by each donor is only $25.

Example 2: Your church invites members to attend a banquet without charge. At the end of the banquet, the members are given the opportunity to donate to the church's mission fund. Those contributions would probably not require *quid pro quo* receipts or disclosure even if the amount given is $75 or more because there not a direct relationship between the meal and the donation.

Auctions: In the eyes of the IRS, there is usually no charitable contribution generated when a bidder purchases an item at a church auction. The IRS generally takes the position that the fair market value of an item is set by the bidders with the purchase price.

However, some tax professionals will advise you that when the purchase price exceeds the fair market value of the items, the amount that exceeds the FMV is deductible as a charitable contribution. If your church takes this position, the *quid pro quo* rules addressed in this section will apply. To comply with those rules, some churches will set the value of every object sold and provide receipts to buyers.

*A **penalty** can be imposed on a church that does not make the required written disclosure in connection with a quid pro quo contribution of more than $75. The penalty can be up to $10 per contribution.*

5.   Donors and the Church's Good Faith Estimate:

In order to determine fair market value, the church must sometimes use their best guess based on the information they have. This best guess is called the *good faith estimate*. A good faith estimate is based on the fair market value of the goods or services received, but sometimes there is room for disagreement. You may have a donor who believes your good faith estimate is wrong. There are two ways a donor may be able to increase the deductible amount above the church's good faith estimate.

1. *Disagreement with the estimate:* A donor may disagree with a church's good faith estimate of the deductible amount. If the donor can justify why he feels the estimate is inaccurate, he may ignore the estimate. The donor must keep any documentation supporting his choice to ignore the estimate for review by the IRS if audited.

2. *Refusal of Benefits:* A full deduction can be claimed by the donor if they refuse the goods or services provided from your church at the time the contribution is made.

For example, if a donor purchases tickets to a church banquet but decides a week later not to go, they still must deduct the value of the tickets from their contribution before claiming a deduction. If he buys the tickets as support for the function, but tells the coordinator he is not coming at the time of purchase, the full amount of the ticket is deductible.

If this is a common situation in your church, consider providing a form with a refusal box the donor can check at the time of his donation to indicate he did not accept the banquet tickets. Perhaps, "*If you cannot attend, please consider a donation of $____.*"

E.   Non-Cash Contributions

Frequently, generous members of your congregation may wish to donate to the church by giving computers, supplies, food, and other useful items. They sometimes also wish to donate things the church does not have a use for. Every church should have a written policy stating they will only accept gifts that can be used by the church, or, if unusable by the church, they can be sold. A written policy gives the pastor or governing council members a graceful way to tell a donor no thank you.

> *In the attic of many a church is a collection of non-cash contributions the church adminsitration didn't know how to refuse.*

1.   Requirements

For non-cash gifts the church is willing to receive, the church is required to give a written receipt. The church is NOT required to establish the value of the item, and no value should be included on the receipt. The following items, however, must be included:

- donor's name
- description of the property, but not the value
- statement declaring if any goods or services were provided to the donor in exchange for the contribution
- a statement regarding the usefulness of the donated property to further the church's tax-exempt purpose
- date and location of the donation
- date the contribution receipt was issued

Donors should be aware that IRS regulations require all donors who make noncash contributions valued *by the donor* at $250 to $500 to obtain a contemporaneous written acknowledgement from the charitable organization. *Contemporaneous* means the taxpayer must have the receipt in their possession at the time they claimed the tax deduction on a timely-filed tax return.

Along with the noncash contribution receipt, the donor should keep:

- how much they claimed as a deduction,
- the fair market value of the property at the time it was donated, and
- the calculation of the fair market value of the property.

> *Extra documentation from your organization is required for donations of vehicles. This is covered in a later section.*

2.   Donations of Property over $500

If donors give your church items valued over $500, there is a bit more paperwork involved for both you and the donor.

Your donors should be aware that for contributions of property valued at more than $500 but less than $5,000, the IRS requires a written acknowledgement as described above, plus the donor's records must include:

- How the donated property was acquired (by purchase, gift, inheritance, exchange, etc.).
- When the donor acquired the property (approximately if exact date not known).
- The cost and any adjustments to the cost basis of donated property held less than 12 months. (Does not apply to publicly traded securities.)

Part of Form 8283 must be completed and attached to a Form 1040 by donors whose total deductions for noncash contributions in a calendar year is over $500.00. Many churches will advise their donors of this obligation and provide Form 8283 as a courtesy with the donor's noncash contribution receipts.

3. Contributions of Property over $5000:

If your church is fortunate enough to receive contributions of property other than money and publicly traded securities with a reported value over $5,000, the DONOR must obtain a qualified appraisal and attach an appraisal summary to the return on which the deduction is claimed. There is an exception for non-publicly traded stock. If the claimed value of the stock does not exceed $10,000 but is greater than $5,000, the donor does not have to obtain an appraisal by a qualified appraiser.

The appraisal summary must be on Form 8283, signed and dated by the church and the appraiser, and attached to the donor's tax return. **The signature by the church does not represent agreement in the appraised value of the contributed property**.

Remember, it is the DONOR's responsibility to file a Form 8283 if required. Your church is under no responsibility to insure the donor files this form or that it is accurately completed. However, advising donors of their responsibility and providing them with the form is a courtesy your church should provide.

4. Church Reporting for Donated Personal Property:

Churches receiving donated property valued at over $5,000 by the donor have two requirements:

- The donor must be given a written noncash acknowledgement. This is a contribution receipt containing the information stated under Requirements, and

- A representative of the church must complete and sign Part IV of Section B of the donor's Form 8283 appraisal summary. Your signature does not represent agreement in the appraised value of the contributed property.

Additionally, your church may be required to file a Form 8282, Donee Information Return, with the IRS if all three of the following conditions occur:

- the church receives a noncash contribution of personal property valued at more than $5,000 by the donor,
- the donor presents your church with a qualified appraisal summary (Form 8283, Section B, Part IV) for signature, and
- the donated property is sold, exchanged, or otherwise disposed of by the church within three years after the date of the contribution.

Form 8282 must be filed **within 125 days** of the date the donated property was sold, exchanged, or otherwise disposed of. A church that receives a charitable contribution valued at more than $5,000 from a corporation generally does not have to complete Form 8283.

Any time you receive property valued over $5000, I'd recommend consulting your local accountant to assure everything is completed and filed correctly.

> ***Important Note:*** *Form 8282 provides detailed information on the contribution and the disposal of the property. A copy of Form 8282 must be provided to the donor and retained by the church.*

5.   Example of Property Donation Acknowledgement

In order to help visualize the acknowledgement, I am including an example from Vickey on the following page. Note that she has thanked the donor, described (but not valued) the property donated, and explained how it will be used for the mission. Additionally, the letter tells the donor what he needs to do to make the donation deductible.

Non-Cash Contribution
Statement

ABC Church

1000 Praise Street

Paradise, State 10001

Noncash Acknowledgment # 10

(All receipts should be numbered for accounting and control purposes)

Dear _____,

Thank you for your contribution of a Lenovo G510 laptop computer in good condition. The laptop is just what is needed for our Youth Center and we will be setting it up and using it immediately.

You did not receive any goods or services in connection with this contribution other than intangible religious benefits.

As you know, we are a qualified 501(c)(3)organization, so if you plan on claiming a tax deduction for this contribution you are responsible for establishing the value of the donated item. Under section 170(f)(8)(b) of the Internal Revenue Code, ABC Church is prohibited from estimating the fair market value of your donated personal property.

For your information, if the value of the item exceeds $500, you will be required to file Form 8283. If the value exceeds $5,000, you may be required to obtain a certified appraisal. Consult your tax preparer for additional details.

Once again, thank you for the much needed donation. May the Lord richly bless the work of your hands as you follow Him.

Sincerely,

_____

Church Treasurer

Date

RETAIN FOR INCOME TAX PURPOSES

F.   Gifts of Autos, Boats, and Airplanes

Sometimes there may be a tax benefit to your donor if they give your church a vehicle instead of selling it themselves and then donating the money. For this reason, churches and other nonprofits often receive gifts of automobiles, boats, or even airplanes.

Before you accept a donation of an automobile, boat, or even an airplane, it is imperative that you understand all of the regulations that guide the acceptance of these types of vehicles. You should make sure your donors understand the regulations as well. A good way to do this is to give them a copy of IRS Publication 4303, *A Donor's Guide to Vehicle Donations.*

If your church has decided to accept the gift, all of the regulations relating to gifts discussed previously apply. IRS Form 1098-C can be used as your written acknowledgement to the donor.

> *If you sell the donated car or other qualified vehicle before you put it to any significant use, the donor's deduction is limited to the gross proceeds of the sale, NOT the fair market value.*

Additionally, your church must provide additional information to the donor, including your intended use of the vehicle **within 30 days of the contribution or the sale of the vehicle**.

The value of the vehicle determines what reporting is required.

1. Donations of Vehicles with Claimed Value less than $500:

Churches are required to provide contemporaneous written acknowledgement for any donation of a car or other qualified vehicle with a claimed value of at least $250. If the claimed value is less than $500, that written acknowledgement *must* include the following information:

- Donor's name,
- Description of the property, but not the value ,
- Statement declaring if any goods or services were provided to the donor in exchange for the contribution, and
- Statement that goods or services provided by the charity consisted entirely of intangible religious benefits, if that was the case.

If your church sells the car without significantly using or improving it **and** for less than $500, your donor can claim a tax deduction equal to or less than the fair market value of the car. The donor is responsible for substantiating the claimed value.

2. **Donations of Vehicles with Claimed Value of more than $500:**

If your church receives a donation of a qualified vehicle with a claimed value of $500 or more, the church must provide the donor with a written acknowledgement within 30 days of the sale of the donated property. If your church plans on keeping and using the vehicle to further its tax exempt purpose, there is a whole other set of regulations we will examine after we look at the regulations regarding sold vehicles.

3. **Sold Donated Vehicles**

The written acknowledgement for *sold donated vehicles* must include the following:

- Name and taxpayer identification number of the donor
- Vehicle, boat, or airplane identification number or similar number
- Date of contribution
- Date of sale
- Gross proceeds from the sale
- Certification that the property was sold in an arm's length transaction (the buyer and seller act independently and have no personal relationship between them).
- A statement that the deductible amount may not exceed the amount of the gross proceeds.
- A statement declaring if any goods or services were provided to the donor in exchange for the contribution.
- A statement that goods or services provided by the charity consisted entirely of intangible religious benefits, if that was the case.

Your church can provide all of this information to the donor using IRS form 1098-C. You can order this form from the IRS by calling 800- TAX-FORM or searching IRS.gov. The church will then need to submit Form 1098-C to the IRS by February 28th of the following year.

As a courtesy to your donors, inform them of the following:

- *The amount of their charitable contribution deduction is limited to the gross proceeds from the sale of their donated vehicle.*

- *No deduction is allowed unless the donor itemizes his deductions on his annual returns rather than using the standard deduction.*

- *The donor will be required to attach IRS Form 8283 and a written acknowledgement or completed Form 1098-C to their tax return.*

- *An appraisal is not required if the donor's deduction is limited to the gross proceeds of the sale.*

4. Vehicles Not Sold:

Your church may plan to significantly use or materially improve a donated auto, boat, or airplane before or instead of selling the property. In such circumstances, your church would not include a dollar amount in the written acknowledgement.

Instead, the written acknowledgement, sent within 30 days of the contribution of the vehicle in order to be considered contemporaneous (i.e. timely), would include the following information:

- Name and taxpayer identification number of the donor
- Vehicle, boat, or airplane identification number or similar number
- Date of contribution
- Statement declaring if any goods or services were provided to the donor in exchange for the contribution
- Statement that goods or services provided by the charity consisted entirely of intangible religious benefits, if that was the case
- Certification and description of the intended use or material improvement of the property and the intended duration of the use
- Certification that the property will not be transferred in exchange for money, other property, or services before completion of such use or improvement

As with the sold vehicles, Form 1098-C may be used as the acknowledgement. Your church will be required to submit Form 1098-C to the IRS by February 28th of the following year. The donor will use the fair market value of their donated vehicle for their tax deduction.

In some circumstances, a car may be sold quite a bit lower than the fair market value or even given to a person in need. In that case, the written acknowledgement must include all of the information detailed above **PLUS**:

- Certification that the church will sell the car at a price significantly below fair market or gratuitously transfer the property to a person in need, and that the sale or transfer will be in the direct furtherance of the church's charitable purpose of relieving the poor and distressed or the underprivileged who are in need of a means of transportation.

See IRS Publication 4302, *A Charity's Guide to Car Donations*, for more details and also how to handle improvements done on the donated vehicle.

G.   Summary — For a Qualified Deduction

In summary, remember, no deduction of an auto, boat, or airplane is allowed unless the donor receives Form 1098-C within 30 days after the date that the vehicle is sold or within 30 days of the donation date if the church keeps the car. If the vehicle is sold, the donor must be informed of the selling price.

If your church decides to keep the car, the fair market value must be used by the donor to figure the charitable tax deduction for the donation, not a higher dealer retail price. One of the best ways for a donor to obtain this information is with a used vehicle pricing guide such as *Kelly Blue Book*.

Be careful—penalties apply to churches that knowingly furnish a false or fraudulent acknowledgement or fail to furnish an acknowledgement in accordance with the time and content requirements.

> *Be certain you understand the church's requirements regarding vehicle donations. The last thing you want is an upset donor who did not receive his tax deduction because the church did not follow the rules!*

VI.   Contributions—Part 3: Other Topics

Most of the time the contributions your church receives are pretty standard. From time to time, contributions of a more personal nature may come up. In this chapter we'll cover how to handle:

- Gifts designated to specific individuals

- Donated labor or services

- Discounts received from vendors

- Checks received but written to another charity

A.   Gifts to Specific Individuals

The members of your church are probably very generous and caring individuals. If they hear of a family in need, they may wish for the church to "pass the hat" through the congregation and give the collection to the family.

Your members need to be aware that any gifts designated to a particular person or family is considered a conduit or pass-through transaction and is not deductible by the donor. The money can be given to the family, but as the family is not a nonprofit organization, the donation is not deductible by the donor, nor should it be included on their contribution summary.

From the IRS:

If contributions to the fund are earmarked by the donor for a particular individual, they are treated, in effect, as being gifts to the designated individual and are not deductible. However, a deduction will be allowable where it is established that a gift is intended by a donor for the use of the organization and not as a gift to an individual. The test in each case is whether the organization has full control of the donated funds, and discretion as to their use, so as to insure that they will be used to carry out its functions and purposes. Revenue Ruling 62-113.

In order for the donation to be deductible, the church must have full control of the funds. This is why it is important to properly set up and administer a benevolence program. See Chapter VII for more details.

If a donor makes gift to the church's music fund, it is an appropriate restriction and therefore deductible. If the donor requests it be given to the organist, it is not deductible as the IRS would consider it a gift to the individual.

1. Before accepting a gift for a specified individual

There are two options to consider before accepting a gift earmarked for a specified individual:

- The first option is to refuse to accept the check. Per IRS publication 3833, donors cannot earmark contributions to a charitable organization for a particular individual or family. You would inform him that his thoughtful gift is very much appreciated, but he needs to give it directly to the designated family or individual as the church does not handle pass-thru contributions.
- The second option would be to accept the check and stamp "NONDEDUCTIBLE" in red ink on the front of the check. That action would let the donor know that he could not use that particular check as a tax deduction with his itemized deductions in his personal income tax forms. Any local office supply store can usually make such a stamp for your church.

If you accept the check, do **not** include the nondeductible contribution on the donor's annual contribution statement. If it is included, there should be a notation indicating that particular gift is not tax-deductible and was not included in their deductible total.

> *If the donor has written a person's name on the check or offering envelope, you should NOT include it in the annual donor acknowledgement report.*

2. Exception for missionaries

There is an exception to the nondeductible issue when it pertains to offerings taken up for missionaries. If the church initiates and controls an offering taken up for a specific missionary, the contribution is tax deductible for the donor and should be included in the donor's contribution receipts. Remember: it all boils down to the church having complete control of funds and using those funds to further its tax- exempt purpose.

B.   Donated Labor/Services

Most churches have members in their congregation who use their professional talents to help out the church. So it is not uncommon to be asked: "Can my church issue a receipt for donated labor and/or services?"

Sadly, the answer to that question is: **No**. The IRS does not permit a tax deduction for donated labor or services. This goes for CPAs, attorneys, and other much appreciated individuals that may generously donate their talent and services to helping a church. A nonprofit or church is **NOT ALLOWED** to issue a contribution receipt for donated labor or services, no matter how valuable that individual's time is.

You can, however, track the value of these services as an *In Kind Donation*. Accounting rules allow you to record the fair market value of professional services, like attorneys and accountants, in an In Kind donation account in the revenue section of the statement of activities. This is more important for nonprofit organizations who need to show potential donors the strength of their total donations.

> *A contribution receipt may be issued for donated materials and other out-of-pocket expenses, but not the donated labor.*

For example, a repairman voluntarily came and fixed your church's air conditioner. He usually charges $75 per hour for his labor and he spent $50 for parts. You can issue him a **NONCASH** contribution receipt for the parts; however, his labor is a generous non-deductible gift to the church. Also, he can deduct his mileage to the church and back if he itemizes deductions on his tax return.

Un-reimbursed expenses that volunteers incur while performing their volunteer services can generally be deducted from their personal tax return. Examples of deductible items include mileage at the current federal standard mileage rate, travel and lodging, and meals incurred during travel which require an overnight stay.

If a volunteer claims a deduction for unreimbursed expenses exceeding $250, they should receive a letter from your church indicating the type of services they provided.

The letter should not include the value of the volunteer's expenses. The burden is upon the volunteer to prove their expenses.

C.   Discount Donations

Local businesses will often give a church a substantial discount on goods or services. Unfortunately, a discount in any form is not considered a qualified charitable contribution for a tax deduction. Your church is **not allowed** to issue a contribution receipt for a discount.

It may make more sense for the landlord or merchant to charge the fair market value and then make a donation to the church for the amount that would be discounted. In this situation, the church would issue a contribution receipt for the donation money.

D.   Checks Written to Another Charity

It is not uncommon for a church to take up an offering for another nonprofit such as a mission organization. Donors may write the check made out to your church with a designation for the other charity or they may write out the check in the other charity's name.

For checks made out to your organization, record them in the donors' records and include the amount on their contribution statements. The church should also set up an accounts payable account for the charity.

If any of the checks were written payable to the other organization, you would not record it in your church's records. The check should be delivered to the other organization, not deposited into the church's bank account.

In this situation, your church would not issue a receipt for that contribution. The other organization would need to issue the acknowledgement to entitle the donor to claim the gift as a charitable contribution.

Also, be aware that donations by U.S. taxpayers to a foreign charity are not eligible for a tax deduction.

E.   Summary

This chapter highlighted some other types of contributions a church may receive. Please keep in mind, the donor's giving statements should NOT include designated gifts for specific individuals (unless it is for a missionary), donated labor or services (though the supplies can be acknowledged), discounts from vendors, or checks made out to another charity. A receipt may be issued for donated materials and out-of-pocket expenses.

VII.   Benevolence Fund

One of the missions of a church is to help care for individuals in its community. Therefore it is not unusual for the members of your church to want to help people with sincere needs. Special collections may be considered for someone dealing with severe medical issues or the need for a new furnace.

These are good and valid deeds, but, as we discussed in the previous chapter, the IRS has very specific rules relating to raising money for a specific individual. Without these rules, unethical people could request a tax deduction for a gift to a relative regardless of their need.

In order to assure your donors can take advantage of tax benefits for donations to those in need and that the recipients are not taxed on the gift, your church should set up a benevolence fund.

> *The strongest reasons for properly setting up a benevolence fund program is to ensure donations to that plan will be considered tax-deductible and payments made to persons in need will not be taxable.*

If you have a proper benevolence policy in place, and all the criteria listed in your policy for helping recipients has been met, you may issue a tax-free benevolence payment.

Without a benevolence policy, the contributions may not be tax-deductible, and in some instances, the church may not even be able to accept offerings that are earmarked for specific individuals. These would be considered pass-thru contributions. IRS publication 3833 states: "*Donors cannot earmark contributions to a charitable organization for a particular individual or family.*"

Therefore, even when your church has a benevolence policy in place, it is unwise to take up a special offering for a particular person. Instead, encourage your members to give to the benevolence fund regularly. Then, the contributions solicited are tax-deductible to the donor.

> *Your pastor can give examples of families who need the benevolence funds, but cannot promise to give the funds to a particular person.*

In this chapter, we'll review:

- The requirements for a benevolence fund
- How to handle a pastor-administered discretionary fund
- Benevolence for employees
- Disbursement procedures
- An example of a benevolence policy

A. Requirements

Individuals, whether a member or not, will often seek out churches when they are in need. The most common requests for benevolence includes: utilities, rent, lodging, food, medical expenses, transportation, and funerals. In order for your church to properly help these individuals, it is imperative for you to have a written policy in place. Your benevolence policy should include requirements that the church must document in writing that all benevolent expenditures meet at least two requirements:

- Need
- Lack of recipient resources

Need is defined as something that is necessary or a necessity. It is up to the church to define *need* in their policy.

You should also include:

- What kinds of need are eligible for benevolence payments.
- Who will make the decision as to what needs the church may or may not assist.

Types of documentation the individual can share with the church to show need include: a cutoff notice from the electric company, a medical bill, or a written memo by a staff employee who has called and verified the need.

The second requirement, **lack of resources**, could be satisfied by reviewing a paycheck stub, their tax return, or a bank statement.

You may wish to have the recipient sign a statement detailing their lack of resources to pay for their need.

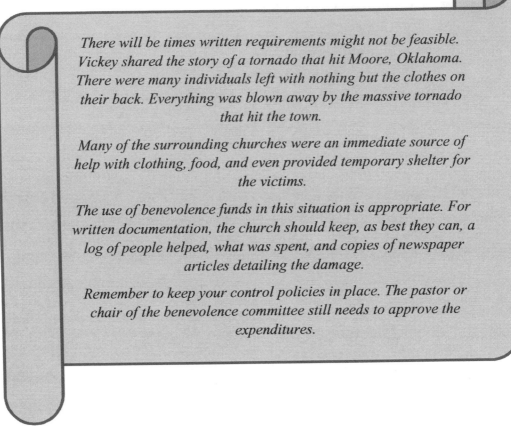

There will be times written requirements might not be feasible. Vickey shared the story of a tornado that hit Moore, Oklahoma. There were many individuals left with nothing but the clothes on their back. Everything was blown away by the massive tornado that hit the town.

Many of the surrounding churches were an immediate source of help with clothing, food, and even provided temporary shelter for the victims.

The use of benevolence funds in this situation is appropriate. For written documentation, the church should keep, as best they can, a log of people helped, what was spent, and copies of newspaper articles detailing the damage.

Remember to keep your control policies in place. The pastor or chair of the benevolence committee still needs to approve the expenditures.

As much as I hate to bring this up, remember there are unscrupulous people and con artists out there. Churches that do not have the resources to verify the need requirements often choose to donate some of their benevolence funds to the local Salvation Army or similar organization. If a person unknown to the pastor comes to the church requesting funds, he can send them to the Salvation Army to be properly vetted and helped as appropriate.

B. Discretionary Benevolence Funds

Benevolence funds may be administered via a committee or set up as a *discretionary benevolence account*. A discretionary benevolence account is administered by the pastor only and has the advantage of allowing the pastor to meet individual's needs privately.

There are special precautions you need to set up to avoid all amounts coming into the fund becoming taxable income to the pastor:

- The minister must account for the expenditures. This can be a checkbook register, spreadsheet, etc. and should be reconciled on a timely basis.
- Written documentation as in the examples above must be required.
- A review of the expenditures needs to be included in your annual audit of the church financials.

C.   Benevolence for Employees

When the individual in need is an employee, the church's gift to them is taxable in most situations. Even though benevolence payments are not normally taxable to the recipient, benevolence payments made to employees are not tax-free. The Internal Revenue Code requires all benevolence payments provided to employees to be considered taxable income and included on the employee's W-2. Furthermore, if the employee is not a minister, you should even withhold all applicable payroll taxes as if the payment were wages.

The same rule applies to expenses paid on behalf of the employee, such as a doctor bill. Benevolence to family members of employees can also be considered income to that employee. If this situation arises, be sure to read Internal Revenue Code Section 102 or talk to a tax specialist.

However, there is an exception to this rule. If an employee suffers losses as a result of a national disaster, the benevolence payments are tax-free, as long as they are for qualifying expenses. The requirements for that exception are quite lengthy, so see *section 139* of the Internal Revenue Code. IRS publication 3833 is available to explain how these requirements work. Please refer to it if your employees are affected.

D.   Earmarked Benevolence Contributions

Even with a benevolence fund set up, contributions to specified individuals are not tax-deductible. The only way the contribution can be considered tax-deductible is for the church to have **full control** over the destination of that gift.

In a nutshell, this means your donor cannot tell you who should receive his funds.

For example, Joe Smith has been laid off for over six months and is struggling to pay his rent. Mary Jones hands you a check with the church's name on it and tells you she wants her check to go to Mr. Smith to help with his rent. Even though Ms. Jones does not have Joe Smith named on the check, she has taken away the church's control of her contribution by specifying verbally that she wants it to go to Mr. Smith.

As we discussed in the previous chapter, the church has the option to decline the donation or to mark it as nondeductible and not include it on the contribution summary.

E. Disbursement Procedures

Whether your benevolence fund is run by a committee or is a discretionary fund managed by the pastor, formal disbursement controls and policies are required. The written documentation discussed in section A must be gathered.

Your church may wish to have a formal request for assistance application in order to assure consistency of the information gathered. The application should be reviewed and collaborated by a church representative.

The committee or pastor reviews the requests and comes to a decision. If approved, the request is signed by the person authorizing the payment. Checks are then written and disbursed. Where possible, the checks should be made payable to vendors, utility companies, hospitals, etc. instead of the individual.

> *Remember:*
>
> *Donors may NOT specify a particular individual or family either on their check or verbally. The church must have full control over the funds.*
>
> *Written documentation of the need is required and saves trouble and heartache.*

F. Written Benevolence Policy Example

You now understand what a benevolence fund is and the importance of having a standard benevolence policy. Next let's examine what the written policy should look like.

Your benevolence policy should include the following wording or something similar (compliments of Vickey Boatright's Freechurchaccounting.com):

ABC Church
Sample Benevolence Policy

In the exercise of its religious and charitable purposes, ABC Church has established a benevolence fund to help individuals in need.

ABC Church members are welcome to suggest individuals that they think would be good candidates for our benevolence fund. Donors may contribute to the fund at any time. However, donors may not specify that their contributions should go to a certain individual. (*Their suggestions can only be just that—suggestions—not requirements of their contributions.*)

ABC Church has full control of administrating its benevolence fund. (Your policy should also spell out who exactly will make the final determination on which applicants will receive payments.)

The purpose of ABC Church's benevolence fund is to meet qualifying individuals' basic needs. (You will need to spell out exactly what kind of assistance your church provides and what it CANNOT provide, when it can be provided, and how the assistance should be provided.)

Check should be made payable to "*ABC Church*" with a notation that the funds are to be placed in the church's benevolence fund.

G.   Summary

The use of a benevolence fund is instrumental for a church. A written policy is crucial, you must require documentation, and do not allow donors to specify a particular individual or family. Disbursements need the proper approval. Employees should not be given benevolence payments without including it in their taxable wages, unless it falls within the natural disaster rules. With a few simple steps, the church can assure donors their contributions are tax deductible and individuals can be helped as needed.

VIII.   Paying the Bills

So far we have covered how to handle the various types of contributions and other money coming in. Now we need to review the systems necessary to pay the bills.

In this chapter we'll cover how to:

- Approve and pay the bills
- Allocate the expenses across programs and funds
- Account for automatic drafts from the checking account and credit card payments
- Replenish the petty cash fund

A.   Terminology

I'd like to review terminology for a moment here just to make sure we are all thinking about the same thing. Accountants like to use the term *vendor* to encompass anyone we owe money to for a good or service. Our employees and donors can also be vendors if we need to reimburse them for an expense. As I refer to vendors throughout this chapter, realize I could be talking about the electric company, the landlord, a supply company, or even a nonprofit the church raised money for.

The term *invoice* is used both with vendors and with donors (or customers). If someone owes the church for a summer day camp, we may send them an invoice asking for the money. When the church buys something from someone else (a vendor), the vendor will send the church an invoice. For this chapter, when I mention invoices, I am referring to those we need to pay (the bills).

Another term you will find me using is *allocations*. Your church probably has a number of different programs, funds, and projects. Each of these may have specific expenses related to them, like copying or postage. As you are paying the bills, you may need to allocate the expenses to different areas.

B.   Approving and Paying the Bills

In Chapter III, we spent some time discussing the chart of accounts. The chart of accounts is the list of items we use to summarize our financial system. As we are paying the bills, we need to be sure we are coding the expenses to the right area in order for our financial system to be correct and to produce detailed reports.

When a bill comes into the church, it should be given to the person who purchased the items for approval. The person should review the bill for accuracy and sign it with a notation explaining which program or project it was for. General church bills (utilities, copier lease, etc.) should be reviewed by the church administrator or the pastor and signed. Once the invoices are approved, they can be given to the bookkeeper to issue the checks.

Bills should not be entered before they are approved. I understand sometimes people aren't always available, so it is tempting to go ahead and print out the checks with the thought, "I'll remind him to approve the invoice when he signs the check,"

But the invoices are often not as well scrutinized when there is a stack of checks waiting to be signed. Additionally, if any corrections need to be made to the bills, the check must be voided and reissued.

To help combat these issues, select one day a week or two specific days a month that checks will be printed. Let all of the staff and volunteers know that if they want a particular bill paid, they need to have it approved and on the bookkeeper's desk by the designated days.

It may take a week or two to train the staff (and expect some complaining), but if you stick to your guns, bill paying will go much smoother on a regular basis.

C.   Scams

Scams are becoming more and more sophisticated. Even the most intelligent people can get caught in scams, and churches are becoming a prime target.

Beware of Scams!

Lynne Albert, a North Carolina attorney, warned me about the increase in calls she has been recieving from churches caught in scams. One of the most egregious scams involved a company calling churches asking for permission to run a free yellow page ad and record their conversation. The church would then be billed for an ad, and when they disputed the bill, the recording was doctored to sound as if it was approved. A credit card was requested to give the church a "break" on the price.

Do Not Ever Give Banking or Credit Card Information to Someone Who Has Called You!

Other common scams are to send bills which look like a normal business's. For example, a bill might be received for office supplies from a familiar-sounding company. If no one can verify they received the supplies, do NOT pay the bill. Charges for copier maintenance and phone line maintenance are also common. Even if you have been paying these, verify you are receiving the service.

Scammers may also set up dummy collection agencies to scare you if you don't pay. Tell them you will be contacting the Federal Trade Commission's Bureau of Consumer Protection (http://www.ftc.gov/bureaus/bureau-consumer-protection), and I doubt they will bother you again. In fact, anytime I receive calls that sound suspicious at home or through work, I tell the person on the line, "This sounds like a scam." You won't believe how quickly they hang up.

If they are legitimate, they will give you a phone number and additional data for you to research the claim. Regardless, do NOT give them a credit card number or confidential data.

As much as I hate to say this, **BE CYNICAL!**

If someone is asking for money, verify the expenditure. Do not be intimidated into giving them information.

D.   Church Insurance and Contracts

It is the responsibility of the administration of the church to assure that risks to the organization are minimized. Many companies carry insurance specifically for churches. Be certain you understand what is and what is not covered under the insurance.

Do you have a van to transport members? If so, is the insurance sufficient? Do you need waivers signed by the riders? Are church-sponsored mission trips to another state covered? What about trips to a third world country? Anytime you will be doing something "out of the ordinary" for your church, contact your insurance company.

Another area I'd like to address is contracts. Contracts are legally binding documents. They bind whoever signs the contract. If your church is incorporated, the contract must be signed in the **Name of the Corporation** (Your Church, Inc.) with **By** _____, Authorized Agent and _____ Title.

If you sign it, John Doe, not John Doe, Director of Your Church, Inc., you may be personally liable.

Even if your church is not incorporated, the contract still needs to be in the organization's name signed by the person and his title. Check with local legal counsel to determine the personal liability in your state.

With any luck, you may have an attorney in your congregation. If so, ask him to review ANY contracts before you sign them. If not, you may incur some legal fees, but you still need to have contracts reviewed by legal counsel.

E.   Entering Data

If you are using a simple spreadsheet like the one Vickey offers at www.freechurchaccounting.com, you will enter the amount of the invoice under the appropriate expense category of the general ledger tabs and key in the check number used to pay the bill.

	A	B	C	D	E	F	G
1			**Name**				
2			**General Ledger**				
3			**January 2014**				
4							
98							
99							
00	2014	Outside Services, Accounting, Legal, etc.					
01		Beginning Balance				-	
02	6/13/14	Office Max	1012	40.00		(40.00)	
03						(40.00)	
04						(40.00)	
05						(40.00)	
06		Total		40.00	-		
07							
08							
09	2021	Office Supplies, stationary, postage, misc.					
10		Beginning Balance				(40.00)	
11		USPS	1013	30.00		(70.00)	
12						(70.00)	
13						(70.00)	
14						(70.00)	
15		Total		30.00	-		
16							
17							

If you are using a computerized accounting program (like QuickBooks), there will be an area to enter invoices from vendors. You will need to setup the vendor and then designate which accounts the expenses go to.

From *QuickBooks for Churches and Other Religious Organizations.*

The computerized program may also allow you to designate the program by assigning a class. Once the checks are written, look at your cash balance and be sure there is enough money left in the checking account to cover the checks.

F.   Allocation of Expenses

If your church would like to track expenses by program, grant, or fund, you have an extra step or two to take. First, decide if the *overhead* expenses will be allocated to the programs. Overhead is the facilities and administrative costs of running the church. The related costs can be allocated based on square footage of the building used by the program, payroll dollars associated to the program, or a myriad of other ways.

Unless you have a grant that covers some overhead costs or the data will help your governing council run the church, I wouldn't go to the trouble of allocating the overhead. For individual bills like supplies or postage, you can allocate them based on actual usage, i.e. the adult education program printed a newsletter and mailed them to its members. In this type of situation, I would recommend allocating if you want a real understanding of the costs to run a particular program.

If you have an off-the-shelf or specialized accounting program, this is easily done on the invoice entry screen. Refer to the manual of your specific program for directions, or my guide if you are using QuickBooks.

If you are using a spreadsheet, you will need to enter the appropriate portion of a single invoice under each of the affected funds. I've shown a screen shot of a five fund worksheet Vickey has designed.

2014 Date	Item Description	Ck#	General		Building		Missions		Vacation BS		Youth		Balance
			Debit (Expenses)	Credit (Income)	Debit (Expenses)	Credit (Income)	Debit (Expenses)	Credit (Income)	Debit (Expenses)	Credit (Income)	Debit (Expenses)	Credit (Income)	Amount of check
Expenses:													
5001	Expense 1												
6/30/14	Electric Company Inc.	1073	10.00		40.00		10.00		10.00		10.00		(60.00)
													(60.00)
													(60.00)
													(80.00)
													(80.00)
	Total		10.00	0.00	40.00	0.00	10.00	0.00	10.00	0.00	10.00	0.00	

Allocated 1/2 to Building with rest evenly to other programs.

G. Bills Drafted out of the Bank Account

It is often convenient to have regular, recurring bills drafted out of the church bank account. These are normally things like utility and phone bills that must be paid monthly for the church to stay open. You will record these just like you would a check, but instead of inputting a check number, you will indicate it is a draft. I often use the date of the draft as part of the number.

The draft amounts should be entered into your general ledger or check register as soon as you know the amounts so you always have an accurate balance in your checking account. They are also necessary to enter for the bank statement to reconcile.

H. Credit Card Payments

In Chapter I, I explained the need to have the credit card receipts tracked by the user and brought to the bookkeeper before the credit card payment is due. The receipts may be brought to the bookkeeper throughout the month so he has an idea how much cash will be required, or they can be all brought in after the statement is received.

Either way, the receipts should be compiled together, documented as to the purpose and the program, and the summary approved by the appropriate church representative.

Your Church Credit Card Receipts				
Your Name		Approved by.		
Month				
Date	Vendor	Purpose	Program	Amount
06/05/2014	Kinkos	Copies for service	Worship	$ 64.95
06/08/2014	Exxon	Gas for Van	Youth	48.68
Total *				113.63
* must agree to credit card bill				

Receipts are attached before bill is approved and paid.

The total must agree with the credit card bill. The individual line items can be entered by fund or program, and then the check can be issued.

I.   Petty Cash Replenishment

As we discussed in Chapter I, Petty Cash is an *imprest* fund, which means the fixed fund is only replenished after the money is spent.

The example from Chapter I is repeated here. Your Church has $100 in their petty cash fund. Throughout the month, various volunteers used the money and brought back the following receipts:

- $9.95 for donuts for the youth group meeting
- $44.37 for gas to take members to the Habitat for Humanity house
- $15.68 for copier paper for the office

The receipts total $70.00. There should be $30.00 of cash also in the drawer. A check for $70.00 should be made out to Your Church with the receipts as the support for the check signer to review. The check can then be cashed and the drawer replenished.

A simple spreadsheet should be maintained. Here is an example:

| | | | Your Church | | | |
| | | | Petty Cash | | | |
Date	Person Requesting Funds	Purpose	Program	$ Out	$ In
01-Jun		To Start Fund			100.00
05-Jun	Mary Smith	Donuts	Youth Group	9.95	
15-Jun	Jack Rios	Gas for Habitat trip	Outreach	44.37	
29-Jun	Liza Jenkins	Copier Paper	Admin	15.68	
	Total			$ 70.00	$ 100.00
	Balance				$ 30.00

Amount of check to replenish.

Should equal cash in drawer.

The check should be written for the amount of the receipts and each of the line items charged to the correct account and program.

J.   Summary

A crucial element of paying the bills is to have an approval process for expenditures. Besides guarding against fraud and waste, approvals allow the administrators of the church to stay on top of activities and cash needs. Bills should be approved before the checks are cut and only approved if someone can verify the expenditure. Contracts need to be in the church's name and signed by an authorized agent with his title. Insurance should be reviewed on a regular basis, especially with the introduction of new programs or projects.

We've covered the basics of recording normal and recurring bills and learned how to allocate the expenses as well as how to handle credit card charges and replenishing the petty cash fund. Next we will go over expense reimbursement policies and procedures, also known as *Accountable Reimbursement Plans*.

IX. Reimbursement Policies and Procedures

During the day-to-day operations, your pastor or other church employees and volunteers probably run to the post office or retail store to pick up necessary items. They may drive to a local hospital to visit a sick member or buy books to help plan their programs or sermons. Theoretically, they would purchase them through a vendor who would send an invoice to the church for payment.

But we all know it is more common for the employee or volunteer to buy the item and then ask for reimbursement from the church. An *accountable reimbursement policy* is a method for claiming and reimbursing professional or business expenses. A written policy is imperative to keep misunderstandings from arising and to assure tax laws are being followed.

> *The rules for employee expense reimbursements are the same for churches and nonprofits as they are for all other businesses.*
>
> *There are not any special rules for churches or nonprofits in relation to employees' business expenses.*

This chapter will explain:

- How to set up a reimbursement policy
- Give an example of a reimbursement policy resolution
- Which expenses can be included and which cannot
- How to reimburse the expense
- How to handle advance payments

A. Setting up a Reimbursement Policy

In order to be accountable, a strong reimbursement policy should:

- Be written. It can be a simple, short paragraph in the form of a resolution or a long, detailed plan as needed depending on your church.
- Be adopted by resolution of the church board.
- Provide payment for only legitimate expenses with a business purpose, incurred solely for the benefit of the paying entity.

- Require proper substantiation of the expense, including a written record made at or near the time of the expenditure, plus documentary evidence, such as receipts.

- Require that the substantiation be submitted to a third party (usually the treasurer), within a reasonable period of time.

B.   Example of a Reimbursement Policy Resolution

The following is an example of a short reimbursement policy resolution designed by Vickey Boatright. Each church should establish their own policy based on its unique needs. All that is really necessary for establishment of a policy is a simple resolution.

ABC Church

Reimbursement Policy Resolution

The following resolution is hereby adopted by the church council/board of _____. It will be effective for the calendar year _____ and all future years unless specifically revoked or superseded.

The church pastor and/or staff will be reimbursed for ordinary and necessary business expenses incurred in the performance of his or her responsibilities when he/she substantiates the amount, business purpose, date, and place of the expense.

This substantiation must be provided to the church treasurer within sixty (60) days of incurring the expense. The individual must return to the church any amounts received in excess of the substantiated expenses within one hundred twenty (120) days of receipt.

The church will not report any properly substantiated reimbursement payments as income on any Form W-2.

_____

Church Title

_____

Church Title

The church may wish to designate certain items which it elects to have covered by this policy, such as travel, continuing education, attendance at annual conference, books, subscriptions, work supplies, robes, etc. There may be a cap or dollar amount on the total reimbursable business expenses that will be paid. The church may also want to require pre-approvals by the treasurer or responsible person of business expenses in excess of $500 (or any other amount deemed appropriate). Any additional requirements should be included in the policy.

C.   Employee Business Expenses to be Included

Employee and volunteers need to understand what expenses are considered a valid business or professional expense. Generally, this would include mileage based on the standard federal rate, tolls and parking, travel expenses, postage, office supplies, as well as professional dues, subscriptions, and certain books. Personal expenses such as dry cleaning and salon services are not valid business expenses.

1.   Examples of Proper Reimbursement Items:

By no means is the following list all-inclusive, but here are more church-specific expenses which are properly reimbursable.

- Reasonable travel and related expenses for attending annual conferences, district meetings, continuing education conferences, etc.
- Trips to preach at another church.
- Trips to visit members at hospitals, nursing homes, or their homes.
- Lunch meetings with officers of the church to discuss church business.
- Supplies for the church office (e.g. paper, pens, notebooks, etc.).
- A computer required for church work.
- Church-related books and periodicals.
- Robes.
- Office furnishings and equipment (e.g. desk, chairs, telephone, etc.).

Review Schedule C of the Form 1040 tax return for other business related (non-personal) expenses allowed.

> *Note: If the church has reimbursed someone for equipment or other non-consumables, the purchased items belong to the church.*

2. Examples of Improper Reimbursement Items:

For further clarification, it is important to recognize what is **not** considered a proper reimbursable item.

- Mileage to church from home for daily work. This is considered personal commuting by the IRS.
- Vacations, including trips to the Holy Land.
- A computer used primarily by family.
- Everyday clothing, including business suits.
- Child care/dependent expenses.
- Housing related expenses, e.g. utilities, furniture, upkeep (though these may be part of the housing allowance—see Chapter XII).

Additionally, your church may designate additional items as non-reimbursable if they do not feel it to be an appropriate use of their members' donations. For example, even if your church uses wine in the service, the governing body may not feel it is an appropriate use of church funds to pay for wine at a going away party for a staff person.

> *Be certain all of the employees of the church, including the pastor, understand appropriate business expenses.*
>
> *One of the most common ways to steal from a church is to use a church credit card or reimbursements for personal items. With a written policy, there will be no dispute on what is allowed and what is not.*

It's time for my soapbox. **Using donated funds to pay for personal items is stealing!** If you are thinking, "but we've always allowed the pastor to pay for personal expenses through the church—it's just part of his compensation," read Chapter XII on minister's compensation packages. If your church pays the minister's personal expenses instead of a larger salary, he is not paying the full amount of his required taxes.

A written compensation plan that adheres to IRS regulations will also protect the pastor. What if the governing board member who gave him permission to pay for personal items through the church leaves the church? The pastor could be exposed to accusations of fraud or theft. Protect your church and your pastor by following regulations and having written policies.

3.   Standard Mileage Rates

The IRS determines the standard mileage rates every year based on a study of fixed and variable costs of operating an automobile, including gas. For 2014, the following rates were in effect:

- Business travel=56 cents per mile. This is the rate to reimburse employees for their church business-related travel. Mileage from your home to the church is considered commuting miles and is not reimbursable.

- Charitable organization travel=14 cents per mile. This is the rate given to your volunteers for any mileage they incur while assisting the church.

- There is also a 23.5 cents per mile allowance for medical or moving purposes for individuals.

*As these allowances change annually, you will need to check **www.irs.gov** and search standard mileage each December for the following year's rates.*

D.   Reimbursing the Expense

Your staff may submit a bill and ask the church to pay it through the normal bill paying process, or they can substantiate the expense and ask your organization to reimburse them.

1.   Required Documentation for Substantiation.

The IRS requires the church to maintain good records and have actual receipts for any expense over $75 and proper documentation to back up expenses. Your church may wish to set a lower limit.

The documentation provided by the requestor must include a description of what was purchased, the amount, the date, the location from where it was purchased, and the business nature of the expense.

The documentation for some requests is obvious. A detailed cash register receipt from the office supply store will have the list of items purchased, the amounts, the date, and the name of the store. The requestor will need to notate on the receipt or an expense report what the business purpose was (i.e. folders purchased for the adult education class project). This information will also help the bookkeeper code the expenses to the correct program.

> *Basic cash register reciepts often fade over time. Consider scanning a copy of the reciept into a computer file to guard against fading. Be sure to organize the scans and BACKUP your data.*

I strongly recommend designing an expense reimbursement request form (like the one below) that is signed by the person requesting the money. It should be reviewed and approved by the appropriate church representative. This assures you have all of the documentation required for the IRS as well as a concise summary for bookkeeping purposes.

2. Example of a simple expense form.

Here is an example of a simple expense form. You may want to add columns for any additional information your particular church may need.

	A	B	C	D	
1		**Your Church**			
2	**Expense Reimbursment Request**				*Must be approved.*
3					
4	Your Name		Approved by:		
5	Month				
6					
7					
8	**Date**	**Vendor**	**Purpose**	**Program**	**Amount**
9	06/06/2014	USPS	Stamps for Graduation Cards	Youth	$ 38.00
10	06/28/2014	Church Supply	Choir robes	Music	178.65
11–23					
24				*Amount of check.*	
25	Total				$ 216.65
26					

3. Sample Mileage Reimbursement

We discussed earlier the standard rate for mileage reimbursement. I find it useful to have a spreadsheet form for the employees to fill out to calculate this amount. Here is an example.

	A	B	C	D	E	F
1		Your Church				
2		Mileage Reimbursment Request				
3		Employees				
4						
5	Your Name			Approved by:		
6	Month			Change annually.		
7	Federal standard rate				$ 0.56	
8						
9	Date	Reason for trip	Destination	Miles driven	Reimbursable Amount	Program
10	15-Jun	Visit Ms. Jones	City Hospital	50	$ 28.00	Outreach
11	29-Jun	Church conference	Greensboro	285	$ 159.60	Admin
12					$ -	
22					$ -	
23					$ -	
24	Total				$ 187.60	
25						
26	NOTE: Mileage from your home to the church office is not reimbursable.					
27						

You may notice in the example above, the church reimbursed an employee $156.80 for a 280 mile or 2-day trip. Sometimes it is less expensive to rent a car and pay for the gas rather than use the reimbursement amounts.

If your church has a lot of long distance travel, I would recommend going to a local car rental and negotiating a rate. Then calculate the breakeven point between reimbursement costs vs the rental car plus gas.

Adopt a policy requiring employees to rent a car if they will be going over 150 (or whatever your breakeven point is) miles.

4.   Volunteer Mileage

The IRS allows people to deduct the miles spent helping a nonprofit (including a church) but at a reduced rate. Currently the rate is 14 cents per mile. If your church would like to know how many miles are being driven by your volunteers, you may ask them to document it for you. A church representative would then sign, and the volunteer would have documentation for their tax purposes.

The volunteer may not be able to afford to donate both their time and their gas. You could use the same form as a reimbursement request. I've attached an example here.

	A	B	C	D	E	F
1		Your Church				
2		Mileage Report				
3		Volunteers				
4						
5	Your Name			Approved by		
6	Month					
7	*Report submitted for		Reimbursement		Documentation	
8	Federal standard rate				$ 0.14	
9						
10	Date	Reason for trip	Destination	Miles driven	Reimbursable Amount	Program
11	04-Jun	Take food to shut ins	various homes around the city	80	$ 11.20	Outreach
12	09-Jun	Church conference	Greensboro	285	$ 39.90	Admin
13					$	
23					$ -	
24					$ -	
25	Total				$ 51.10	
26						
27	*Use this report to receive a signed document from the church agreeing with your donated miles or to request reimbursement of your mileage expense.					
28	Please note: If you are reimbursed for your mileage by the church, you cannot deduct the mileage from your taxes.					

Note the form asks if it is for reimbursement or documentation purposes. It also explains to the volunteer that if they are reimbursed, they can't request the deduction from their taxes.

Save Time, Avoid Headaches!

These spreadsheets and the example forms are available for purchase in reusable spreadsheet and word processing documents at www.accountantbesideyou.com. Vickey and I understand the monetary restraints of churches, so we give you all of the data for you to design them yourself, but if you'd like to save time, please check out accountantbesideyou.com.

5. Timing

The IRS requires that all substantiation of expenses occur within a "reasonable" time of the expense being paid or incurred. This should be included in the resolution and/or detailed policy plan. A reasonable time frame would be 30 or 60 days.

If your pastor and employees have smart phones, you may want to research the apps available for tracking expenses (and time if that would help). Then design your expense reimbursement forms and requirements around the app's capabilities for a more efficient data flow.

E. Advance Payments

If your staff or volunteers travel, your church may need to issue advance payments for expenses. This can be handled in a couple of different ways.

The first is to estimate the employee's expenses and issue him a check for that amount. The employee will then keep track of eligible expenses and reimburse the church for any amount exceeding the total of the business expenses. If the advance was not sufficient, the church would reimburse the employee for the remaining amount.

In this case, all of the receipts must be given to the church with the request for additional reimbursement or with the leftover funds. This must be done within a "reasonable" amount of time (as defined in your policy).

The second approach is to use the federal per diem rates. These can be found at www.gsa.gov. You can type in a city or zip code, and the government will give you the standard rate for meals and lodging. The meals are then broken down to breakfast, lunch, dinner, and incidentals. If an employee will be gone for two days to a town with a meal per diem of $46, you would issue an advance of $92. As you are using the government rates, you don't need to have them bring back receipts, but they should keep them for their records.

Many business and churches use a combination of per diem advances and reimbursements. For example, they may pay for meals on a per diem basis, but require hotel rooms to be reimbursed.

> *Per the IRS, the first and last day of travel should be calculated at 75% of the per diem rate.*

If your minister's compensation package includes a flat amount paid to him for accountable expenses like gas or books, define how frequently the expense documentation must be provided to the church. Failure to maintain and provide the documentation may cause the advance to be treated as taxable income. See Chapter 12 on Minister's Compensation for more details.

F.   Ticketless Airline Expenses

It is unusual to see an airline ticket anymore. The boarding passes are sometimes even sent as a text message to the traveler's smart phone. But that doesn't mean the documentation isn't necessary.

An email from the airline or travel agency showing the date, place, and cost of the ticket can be used. Attach it to the credit card receipt form or the reimbursement request form with the business reason for the trip.

G.   Ramifications of Not Following the Policy

If a minister or church is audited and there is not proper supporting documents backing up the reimbursement claims, the reimbursements could be considered income for the minister or staff member. They would then owe penalties for not claiming the income, and it could snowball from there.

Do NOT give any left-over funds in your accountable reimbursement plan to any staff person, including the minister, at the end of the year. It would null and void your whole policy, and you would have to include all reimbursements for the year on a W-2 as income. If the church has more cash at the end of the year than expected and wants to reward the employees, treat it as a bonus, not part of the accountable reimbursement plan.

H. Inability to Reimburse a Valid Expense

There may be times when an employee incurs a valid expense, but the church simply cannot afford to reimburse the employee. In a 2012 court case, Stidham, T.C. Summ. Op. 2012-61, the court ruled that a taxpayer is not entitled to take a tax deduction for unreimbursed businesses expenses **if** the employer has a reimbursement policy.

You may need to amend your accountable reimbursement plans to include wording requiring the church to send a written reply to the requesting employee recognizing their claim as legitimate, but denying it on the basis that it cannot afford to issue the reimbursement. This will allow your employee to take the deduction if they cannot be reimbursed.

I. Summary

A written reimbursement plan is a necessary tool for employees and volunteers to understand what is reimbursable and at what rate. It keeps misunderstandings and hard feelings from occurring. And, as importantly, it keeps employees from accidentally incurring taxable income.

Some of the important rules to remember with your Accountable Reimbursement Plan are:

- Define appropriate businesses expenses.
- Inform employees of time limits for requesting reimbursement.
- Get supporting documents such as receipts and mileage logs.
- All documentation must include who, what, when, where, and why.
- Have forms approved.
- Properly file them.
- Appoint someone to be in charge of administrating the accountable reimbursement plan.

It's time to move on to the biggest expense for most churches—Payroll.

X. Payroll—Part I: Basic Steps

For many churches, payroll is the largest expense item. It is also one you want to get perfect every time as it affects your employees and legal situation. In this chapter, I'll start out explaining the terminology and list the forms required. I'm doing this first so you can bookmark the page and refer back to it anytime you don't understand which form I'm referring to.

Later in the chapter, I'll take you through the steps necessary to set up the payroll. Chapter XI will explain how to calculate, pay and file the necessary taxes and forms, and Chapter XII will detail how to handle the minister's payroll.

A. Terminology

When dealing with employees and payroll, there are numerous terms you may hear bantered about. I'll summarize a few.

Gross Pay—Total amount earned in a pay period by an employee before withholding taxes.

Net Pay—The paycheck amount the employee takes home after withholding taxes.

EIN (Employers Identification Number)—Before you start hiring employees or open a bank account, you will need an EIN. It is the number that will identify your organization to the IRS, like the Social Security Number (SSN) does for an individual.

Employees—Persons you pay for their work. They may be paid based on an hourly rate or a set salaried amount.

Independent Contractors—These are people you pay to do a particular job. Taxes are not withheld. Be careful who you classify as independent contractors versus employees as the IRS frowns upon (and punishes) organizations who try to treat employees as independent contractors. We'll go over this in more detail later.

Pay Period—The frequency with which you pay your employees. It may be weekly, semi-monthly, bi-monthly, or monthly.

Exemptions—These determine the amount of taxes withheld and are determined based on marital status, children, and other employee-specific need.

Taxable Wages—May not be the total amount paid to an employee, but the amount of wages paid that taxes will be withheld upon.

Withholding—The federal, state and/or local income taxes withheld from an employee's check.

Social Security and Medicare Tax Withholding—The amount withheld from the employee's check for Social Security and Medicare. The Social Security portion is also referred to as FICA (Federal Insurance Contribution Act).

Employer Taxes or Match—The employer's share of Social Security and Medicare taxes.

Dual Status—A minister is considered an employee for federal income tax purposes and self-employed for Social Security and Medicare purposes.

Unemployment Tax—A payment to a state or federal government to cover unemployed workers. Churches are exempt from federal unemployment taxes, but requirements vary by state.

Workers' Compensation—Money paid to a state to fund support for workers hurt on the job. Most states require workers' compensation, so you will need to check with your state agency.

Disability Insurance Program—is only required in a few states. If you live in California, Hawaii, New Jersey, New York, Rhode Island, or Puerto Rico contact your state's appropriate agency to see if this applies.

Housing Allowance—Ministers are allowed to receive money tax free to the extent of their housing costs. We will cover this in detail in the next chapter.

EFTPS—is the Electronic Federal Tax Payment System. It allows employers to submit the taxes and withholding electronically.

Self-Employment Taxes—A minister and any other self-employed person must file and pay quarterly the Social Security and Medicare taxes at the rate of both the employee and employer. In 2014, this was 12.4% and 2.9% respectfully.

That sums up a few of the terms you may not be familiar with. I'll try to define others as we go. Next, I'd like to describe the various forms you may be using.

B. Forms & Publications

Form Number	Description	Due Date
SS-4	Application for EIN	before hiring employees
IRS Pub. 15 Circular E	The Employers Tax Guide	
W-4	Employee's Social Security Number and allowances being claimed	when employee is hired
I-9	Employment Eligibility Verification—employee must present documents proving citizenship or work permit.	before hiring
941	Employer's Quarterly Federal Tax Return— summarizes the income, Social Security, and Medicare taxes withheld and paid to the government during the previous quarter.	Due the last day of the month following the quarter end. 1st qtr—April 30 2nd qtr—July 31 3rd qtr—October 31 4th qtr—January 31
W-2	Wage and Tax Statement— showing total earnings and taxes withheld. It is used by employees to fill out their tax returns.	by January 31 of the following year
W-3	Transmittal of the W-2. This is the summary form sent to the IRS with copies of all of the W-2s.	by the end of February
1099 Misc	Shows total amount paid to independent contractors over $600 that year.	end of January the following year
W-9	Form completed by independent contractor with their SSN or EIN. Used to fill out the 1099 Misc.	when hiring the independent contractor
1096	Transmittal form for the 1099 Misc.	by the end of February in the following year
1040 ES	Estimated taxes for ministers. This is filed by the minister, not by the church.	Due the 15th of the month following the quarter end. 1st qtr—April 15 2nd qtr—July 15 3rd qtr—October 15 4th qtr—January 15

For your convenience, I've included a page of links to the IRS forms on my website, www.accountantbesideyou.com.

C. Setting up the Payroll

In this section, I'll take you step-by-step through the process of setting up your payroll.

1. EIN—Employer Identification Number

Whether you have started hiring employees or opening a bank account, your church will need an EIN. The EIN is easy to obtain. Go to the IRS.gov website and search for SS-4. The government will even allow you to apply over the phone, but you'll still want to have filled out the form to assure you have all of the information.

On the next page, there is a copy of the actual form. It is fairly easy to follow, so I'll just go over the highlights with you.

Line 1: The **legal name** must tie to any filings you have with your state government. This is not the place to abbreviate your church's name.

Line 2: The **trade name** is only filled in if the church uses a name different from their legal name in the normal course of doing business. If not, leave it blank.

Line 3: Will probably be blank for a church.

Lines 4-6: The address of the church.

Line 7a: The name of the **responsible party** should be the pastor, the governing council's president, or other legal representative of the church. His SSN will be required.

Line 8: No

Line 9a: Asks for the **type of entity**. Select *Church*.

Line 10: Your **reason for applying** will probably be either: started new business, hired employees, or banking purpose.

Line 11: Date your church started.

Line 12: The **closing month of the accounting year**. This is usually December, but many churches have a June year end.

Line 13: Your **expected number of employees** will be listed under *Other*.

Line 14: Allows you to request only **filing payroll reports annually** instead of quarterly if tax liability is expected to be under $1000 for the year. If you have few employees, this may be an option, especially as a church does not pay self-employment tax on the pastor.

Form SS-4
(Rev. January 2010)
Department of the Treasury
Internal Revenue Service

Application for Employer Identification Number
(For use by employers, corporations, partnerships, trusts, estates, churches, government agencies, Indian tribal entities, certain individuals, and others.)
▶ See separate instructions for each line. ▶ Keep a copy for your records.

OMB No. 1545-0003

EIN

1	Legal name of entity (or individual) for whom the EIN is being requested

Type or print clearly.

2 Trade name of business (if different from name on line 1)	**3** Executor, administrator, trustee, "care of" name
4a Mailing address (room, apt., suite no. and street, or P.O. box)	**5a** Street address (if different) (Do not enter a P.O. box.)
4b City, state, and ZIP code (if foreign, see instructions)	**5b** City, state, and ZIP code (if foreign, see instructions)
6 County and state where principal business is located	
7a Name of responsible party	**7b** SSN, ITIN, or EIN

8a Is this application for a limited liability company (LLC) (or a foreign equivalent)? ☐ Yes ☐ No
8b If 8a is "Yes," enter the number of LLC members ▶

8c If 8a is "Yes," was the LLC organized in the United States? ☐ Yes ☐ No

9a Type of entity (check only one box). Caution. If 8a is "Yes," see the instructions for the correct box to check.

☐ Sole proprietor (SSN) _____
☐ Partnership
☐ Corporation (enter form number to be filed) ▶ _____
☐ Personal service corporation
☐ Church or church-controlled organization
☐ Other nonprofit organization (specify) ▶ _____
☐ Other (specify) ▶

☐ Estate (SSN of decedent) _____
☐ Plan administrator (TIN) _____
☐ Trust (TIN of grantor) _____
☐ National Guard   ☐ State/local government
☐ Farmers' cooperative   ☐ Federal government/military
☐ REMIC   ☐ Indian tribal governments/enterprises
Group Exemption Number (GEN) if any ▶

9b If a corporation, name the state or foreign country (if applicable) where incorporated | State | Foreign country

10 Reason for applying (check only one box)
☐ Started new business (specify type) ▶ _____
☐ Hired employees (Check the box and see line 13.)
☐ Compliance with IRS withholding regulations
☐ Other (specify) ▶

☐ Banking purpose (specify purpose) ▶ _____
☐ Changed type of organization (specify new type) ▶ _____
☐ Purchased going business
☐ Created a trust (specify type) ▶ _____
☐ Created a pension plan (specify type) ▶ _____

11 Date business started or acquired (month, day, year). See instructions.
12 Closing month of accounting year

13 Highest number of employees expected in the next 12 months (enter -0- if none). If no employees expected, skip line 14.

14 If you expect your employment tax liability to be $1,000 or less in a full calendar year and want to file Form 944 annually instead of Forms 941 quarterly, check here. (Your employment tax liability generally will be $1,000 or less if you expect to pay $4,000 or less in total wages.) If you do not check this box, you must file Form 941 for every quarter. ☐

Agricultural	Household	Other

15 First date wages or annuities were paid (month, day, year). Note. If applicant is a withholding agent, enter date income will first be paid to nonresident alien (month, day, year) ▶

16 Check one box that best describes the principal activity of your business.
☐ Construction   ☐ Rental & leasing   ☐ Transportation & warehousing
☐ Real estate   ☐ Manufacturing   ☐ Finance & insurance
☐ Health care & social assistance   ☐ Wholesale-agent/broker
☐ Accommodation & food service
☐ Other (specify)

Religious activities.

17 Indicate principal line of merchandise sold, specific construction work done, products produced, or services provided.

18 Has the applicant entity shown on line 1 ever applied for and received an EIN? ☐ Yes ☐ No
If "Yes," write previous EIN here ▶

Third Party Designee
Complete this section only if you want to authorize the named individual to receive the entity's EIN and answer questions about the completion of this form.
Designee's name
Address and ZIP code
Designee's telephone number (include area code) ( )
Designee's fax number (include area code) ( )

Under penalties of perjury, I declare that I have examined this application, and to the best of my knowledge and belief, it is true, correct, and complete.
Name and title (type or print clearly) ▶
Applicant's telephone number (include area code) ( )
Applicant's fax number (include area code) ( )
Signature ▶
Date ▶

Line 15: List the date of your first expected payroll.

Line 16: Asks for your **activities.** Select *Other* and specify *Religious or Church* activities.

Line 17: Services offered would be *Religious Services.*

Line 18: If the church had previously applied for an EIN, note it here.

The form should then be signed, dated, and mailed or faxed to the IRS. Find the current mailing address on their website.

2.   State and Local Identification Numbers

Once you have your federal number, you will need to apply for any state and, possibly, local numbers. Check your state's Secretary of State or Department of Revenue websites for state requirements. It is rare, but your city or county may have additional requirements.

3.   Independent Contractor versus an Employee

You probably already understand what an employee is. An independent contractor is a little less clear. From the IRS website:

> *People such as doctors, dentists, veterinarians, lawyers, accountants, contractors, subcontractors, public stenographers, or auctioneers who are in an independent trade, business, or profession in which they offer their services to the general public are generally independent contractors. However, whether these people are independent contractors or employees depends on the facts in each case. The general rule is that an individual is an independent contractor if the payer has the right to control or direct only the result of the work and not what will be done and how it will be done. The earnings of a person who is working as an independent contractor are subject to Self-Employment Tax.*

The key passage above is **if the payer has the right to control or direct only the result of the work and not what will be done and how it will be done**. In the simplest terms, this means you hire someone to do something and pay them when it is finished.

The IRS assumes individuals working for the church are employees unless it is proven otherwise. When auditing an organization, they have a list of 20 questions to determine if the worker is an independent contractor or not.

Revival ministers, supply preachers and guest speakers are usually classified as independent contractors and should be issued a 1099 if the total paid to them in the year was over $600.

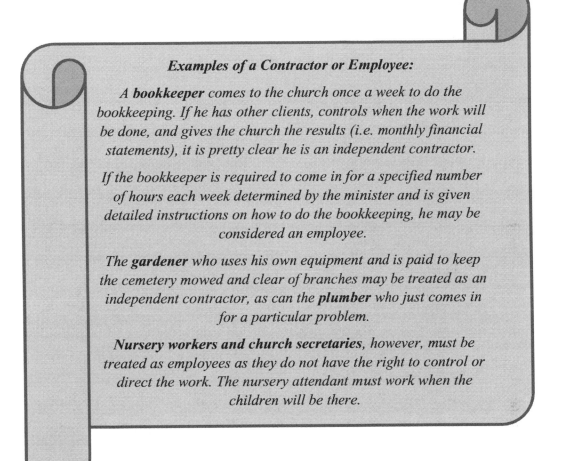

Examples of a Contractor or Employee:

A **bookkeeper** comes to the church once a week to do the bookkeeping. If he has other clients, controls when the work will be done, and gives the church the results (i.e. monthly financial statements), it is pretty clear he is an independent contractor.

If the bookkeeper is required to come in for a specified number of hours each week determined by the minister and is given detailed instructions on how to do the bookkeeping, he may be considered an employee.

The **gardener** who uses his own equipment and is paid to keep the cemetery mowed and clear of branches may be treated as an independent contractor, as can the **plumber** who just comes in for a particular problem.

Nursery workers and church secretaries, however, must be treated as employees as they do not have the right to control or direct the work. The nursery attendant must work when the children will be there.

Direct payment to traveling evangelists or missionaries would also receive a 1099-MISC if the annual amount provided to the individual is $600 or greater. $600 was the IRS limit in 2014. The filing requirement amount should be verified each year.

In case you are wondering why it matters, income tax and payroll taxes are withheld on employees but not independent contractors. Independent contractors have to pay the full (employee and employer) Social Security and Medicare taxes on their earnings. Businesses sometimes like to classify workers as independent contractors to save on the additional employer payroll taxes.

4. W-9 Request for Taxpayer Identification Number

If you have determined the person should be paid as an independent contractor, you will need to have him complete a W-9 Request for Taxpayer Identification Number. The form may be downloaded from the IRS website, http://www.irs.gov/pub/irs-pdf/fw9.pdf.

The contractor fills out the form with his own name or his business name, if applicable. He checks his type of business organization and his address. If he used his personal name, the SSN area should be completed. If he filled the form out as a business, he should use an EIN, if he has one.

The form must be signed and dated and given to the church. I require contractors to fill out the form before I will give them a check for their services.

> *You only need this form if you expect to pay the contractor at least $600 throughout the year. If you aren't sure, go ahead and have him complete it, so you won't have to track it down at year end.*

5. Determine Pay Period

Now that you know who you will be paying as an employee, you should determine how often you will pay them. This is referred to as the pay period.

From an efficiency standpoint, the less frequently, the better. But it is often hard to go an entire month between paychecks, so most organizations pay either bi-monthly (15th and the end of the month) or bi-weekly (every two weeks). Weekly payroll is also an option, but requires more bookkeeping time and costs.

6. Employee Forms I-9 and W-4

Before an employee can be hired, the church must determine if he is legally able to work in this country. An I-9 Employment Eligibility Verification form is required and must be completed by every employee.

Employment Eligibility Verification

Department of Homeland Security
U.S. Citizenship and Immigration Services

USCIS
Form I-9
OMB No. 1615-0047
Expires 03/31/2016

►START HERE. Read instructions carefully before completing this form. The instructions must be available during completion of this form. ANTI-DISCRIMINATION NOTICE: It is illegal to discriminate against work-authorized individuals. Employers CANNOT specify which document(s) they will accept from an employee. The refusal to hire an individual because the documentation presented has a future expiration date may also constitute illegal discrimination.

Section 1. Employee Information and Attestation *(Employees must complete and sign Section 1 of Form I-9 no later than the first day of employment, but not before accepting a job offer.)*

Last Name *(Family Name)*	First Name *(Given Name)*	Middle Initial	Other Names Used *(if any)*

Address *(Street Number and Name)*	Apt. Number	City or Town	State	Zip Code

Date of Birth *(mm/dd/yyyy)*	U.S. Social Security Number	E-mail Address	Telephone Number

I am aware that federal law provides for imprisonment and/or fines for false statements or use of false documents in connection with the completion of this form.

I attest, under penalty of perjury, that I am (check one of the following):

☐ A citizen of the United States

☐ A noncitizen national of the United States *(See instructions)*

☐ A lawful permanent resident (Alien Registration Number/USCIS Number): _____

☐ An alien authorized to work until (expiration date, if applicable, mm/dd/yyyy) _____ . Some aliens may write "N/A" in this field.
(See instructions)

Some aliens may write "N/A" on the Foreign Passport Number and Country of Issuance fields. *(See instructions)*

Signature of Employee:	Date *(mm/dd/yyyy)*:

The employee fills out the first section (shown), then the employer reviews his documents and completes the second section. A list of approved documents is available in the instructions included with the form.

Once the documents are reviewed and the paper is signed by both the employer and the employee, a W-4, Employee's Withholding Allowance Certificate, is given to the employee to be completed.

The employee calculates the recommended number of allowances based on marital status and children to compute a guideline for the number of exemptions he would like. The number of allowances determines how much federal tax is withheld from his check.

A new W-4 needs to be completed anytime an employee's marital status or number of dependents change.

The employee is not required to use the number on the worksheet. If he has large deductible expenses outside this job, he may wish to have less money withheld.

Likewise, if he had a large tax bill the previous year and expects to have another, he may wish to have additional money taken from his check. If not enough money is withheld, the employee may have to pay a penalty. On the other hand, if too much is withheld, the employee has lost the use of those funds and any potential interest for the year.

Once completed, the employee must sign and date the W-4. This is the federal form only. If your state has a state income tax, there is probably a state exemption certificate to be filled out also.

> *Always do a criminal background check before hiring a new employee! This is especially important if the person will be working with children or the finances. It is not expensive and can save the church embarrassment and extra work later.*

7.   Establish Your Payroll Records

For federal tax purposes, you must keep the following information on file:

- the name, address, and SSN of each employee
- the total amount and date of each payment
- the portion of each payment that constituted taxable wages
- each employee's I-9
- each employee's W-4
- copies of returns you filed
- copies of any undeliverable W-2 forms

As this information has confidential data such as SSNs and salary information, it must be kept in a locked, secure file. If you are keeping the information electronically, it needs to be securely password protected.

D. Summary

In order to set up your payroll, you need to apply for an EIN, determine if a person is an employee or an independent contractor, run a criminal background check, determine a pay period, and have the employees fill out the necessary forms. You now understand the basic terminology and what is required. Let's learn how to calculate and pay the payroll.

XI. Payroll — Part II: Calculating & Filing

Now comes the fun part—actually calculating the payroll. You can use a payroll service, but it really isn't too hard to do yourself. First thing you need is to get a copy of the IRS Publication 14 (Circular E). It is available online at IRS.gov or at the local IRS office.

> *Ministers are treated a little differently than other employess. First, I'd like you to understand how regular payroll taxes are computed. I will walk through how to handle minister's payroll in the next chapter.*

Payroll federal tax withholding can be calculated by one of two methods, the tax table or percentage method. The tax table method uses the tax tables listed in the back of Circular E. They are listed by pay period and marital status and show the amount of withholding required by number of allowances. The percentage method uses the schedules in the back of Circular E to compute the withholding.

In this chapter, I'll show you how to:

- Calculate taxes based on both methods
- Calculate Social Security and Medicare taxes
- Compute the employee's paycheck
- Post the payroll expense in the general ledger
- Handle tax deposits and filings
- Handle the year-end requirements

A. Tax Table Method

I think an example will explain this method best. Assume you have a church administrator who is single and has requested two withholding allowances on her W-4. Because you pay biweekly, go to the schedule titled **Single Persons— Biweekly Payroll Period.**

SINGLE Persons—BIWEEKLY Payroll Period

(For Wages Paid through December 2014)

And the wages are—		And the number of withholding allowances claimed is—							
At least	But less than	0	1	2	3	4	5	6	7
		The amount of income tax to be withheld is—							
$800	$820	$91	$68	$45	$27	$12	$0	$0	$0
820	840	94	71	48	29	14	0	0	0
840	860	97	74	51	31		0	0	0
860	880	100	77	54	33	18		0	0
880	900	103	80	57	35	20			0
900	920	106	83	60	38	22	6	0	0
920	940	109	86	63	41	24	8	0	0
940	960	112	89	66	44	26	10	0	0
960	980	115	92	69	47	28	12	0	0
980	1,000	118	95	72	50	30			
1,000	1,020	121	98	75					0
1,020	1,040	124	101	78	56				0
1,040	1,060	127	104	81					0
1,060	1,080	130	107	84					0
1,080	1,100	133	110	87				9	0
1,100	1,120	136	113	90	68	45	26	11	0
1,120	1,140	139	116	93	71	48	28	13	0
1,140	1,160	142	119	96	74	51	30	15	0
1,160	1,180	145	122	99	77	54	32	17	2
1,180	1,200	148	125	102	80	57	34	19	4

Use the column with the number of allowances from the W-4.

The amount to be deducted from the check.

There are columns listing the number of withholdings across the top. The two left columns are the range of wages paid. So if your administrator was paid $1050 for the two week period, you would follow the line starting with 1,040 to the column under 2 allowances. The table shows the federal income tax withholding to be $81.

If the administrator was married, the next chart in the circular, **Married Persons—Biweekly Payroll Period**, would be used instead.

B.   Percentage Method

The second approach is to use the percentage method. In this method, you will multiply the withholding allowance from the table in Circular E times the number of allowance on the W-4. This amount is deducted from the *gross wages* to find *taxable wages*. Gross wages are the total amount the employee earned before any taxes are taken out. Taxable wages are the gross wages less withholding allowance.

Table 5. Percentage Method—2014 Amount for One Withholding Allowance

Payroll Period	One Withholding Allowance
Weekly	$ 76.00
Biweekly	151.90
Semimonthly	164.60
Monthly	329.20
Quarterly	987.50
Semiannually	1,975.00
Annually	3,950.00
Daily or miscellaneous (each day of the payroll period)	15.20

To illustrate computing taxable wages, look at our previous example. The administrator had two allowances, so we will reduce her wages by the allowance amount times 2 or $303.80. Her taxable income is $1050.00-303.80=$746.20.

In order to calculate the federal income tax withholding, look in the Circular E on the **Percentage Method Tables for Income Tax Withholding (for 2014 it** is on page 43). Find the table with the correct pay period, in this case, Biweekly Table 2. Under the **Single Person** column are the wage ranges.

Percentage Method Tables for Income Tax Withholding

(For Wages Paid in 2014)

TABLE 1—WEEKLY Payroll Period

$750	— $1,762 . .	$97.75 plus 25%	—$750	$1,552	-$5,525 . .	$15.40 plus 25%	— $1,762
$1,762	—$3,627 . .	$350.00 plus 28%	—$1,762	$3,025	—$4,525 . .	$556.15 plus 28%	—$3,025
$3,627	—$7,834 . .	$872.20 plus 33%	—$3,627	$4,525	—$7,953 . .	$976.15 plus 33%	—$4,525
$7,834	—$7,865 . .	$2,260.51 plus 35%	—$7,834	$7,953	—$8,963 . .	$2,107.39 plus 35%	—$7,953
$7,865	. . . .	$2,271.36 plus 39.6%	—$7,865	$8,963	. . . .	$2,460.89 plus 39.6%	—$8,963

TABLE 2—BIWEEKLY Payroll Period

(a) SINGLE person (including head of household)—				(b) MARRIED person—			
If the amount of wages (after subtracting withholding allowances) is:		The amount of income tax to withhold is:		If the amount of wages (after subtracting withholding allowances) is:		The amount of income tax to withhold is:	
Not over $87 . . . . $0				Not over $325 . . . . $0			
Over—	But not over—		of excess over—	Over—	But not over—		of excess over—
$87	—$436 . .	$0.00 plus 10%	—$87	$325	—$1,023 . .	$0.00 plus 10%	—$325
$436	—$1,506 . .	$34.90 plus 15%	—$436	$1,023	—$3,163 . .	$69.80 plus 15%	—$1,023
$1,506	—$3,523 . .	$195.40 plus 25%	—$1,506	$3,163	—$6,050 . .	$390.80 plus 25%	—$3,163
$3,523	—$7,254 . .	$699.65 plus 28%	—$3,523	$6,050	—$9,050 . .	$1,112.55 plus 28%	—$6,050
$7,254	—$15,667 . .	$1,744.33 plus 33%	—$7,254	$9,050	—$15,906 . .	$1,952.55 plus 33%	—$9,050
$15,667	—$15,731 . .	$4,520.62 plus 35%	—$15,667	$15,906	—$17,925 . .	$4,215.03 plus 35%	—$15,906
$15,731	. . . .	$4,543.02 plus 39.6%	—$15,731	$17,925	. . . .	$4,921.68 plus 39.6%	—$17,925

With the $746.20 of taxable income, we need to look at the line with **Over $436, But not over $1506**. The tax can be calculated as follows:

- Start with the taxable income of $746.20

- Subtract $436.00 (the amount in the right column titled **of excess over**) to equal $310.20

- Multiply the $310.20 by 15% (the percentage in the middle column **The amount of income tax to withhold is:**). This equals $46.53.

- Add $34.90 from the column **The amount of income tax to withhold is:** to the $46.53 to total $81.43.

This employee's federal withholding is $81.43. You will need to calculate the withholding for each employee. Both methods give you the same tax, so use whichever is easiest for you.

C.   State Tax Withholding

No matter which method you choose, the formulas above are for the federal withholding only. If your state has a state income tax, you will need to do a similar calculation with your state withholding rates. Check your state's Department of Revenue website or office for more information.

D.   FICA—Social Security & Medicare Taxes

The Federal Insurance Contributions Act (FICA) is a federal system of old-age, survivors, disability, and hospital insurance. The old-age, survivors, and disability insurance part is financed by the Social Security tax while the hospital insurance part is financed by the Medicare tax.

The taxes are required to be withheld on all part-time and full-time employees (except ministers as we will discuss in the next chapter). Once an employee is paid $117,000, you no longer need to withhold Social Security tax on the excess, but you will continue withholding for the Medicare portion of the tax. Any earnings over $117,000 are not taxed with Social Security because the benefits are capped to that earning rate.

The Social Security tax rate is 6.2% to be withheld from the employee and 6.2% matched by the employer. So the total Social Security tax is 12.4% (in 2014) of the employee's wages without withholding allowances, equally split between the employer and employee.

The Medicare rate is 1.45% of the employee's wages without withholding allowances each for the employee and employer. If you pay an employee over

$200,000 per year, you will need to withhold an additional .9% for **Additional Medicare Tax**. There is no employer match to the .9%.

Let me walk you through the SS and Medicare tax withholding calculation using the earlier example. The administrator had $1050 of gross earnings. To calculate his taxes,

- Multiply $1050 times 6.2% to equal $65.10 for SS.

- Multiply $1050 times 1.45% to equal $15.23 for Medicare.

- Reduce his paycheck by $80.33 ($65.10 +$15.23).

Additionally, the church will need to calculate its employer tax liability by multiplying the gross wages by the employer tax percentages.

- Add the 6.2% for SS tax to 1.45% for Medicare to equal 7.65% employer tax percentage

- Multiply gross wages of $1050 times 7.65% to equal $80.33 of employer tax liability.

Now you have enough information to prepare the employee's paycheck.

E. The Employee's Payroll Check

Once all of the deductions have been calculated, you will need to compute the net amount due to the employee. I like to do this in a spreadsheet to make it easier to double check my calculations and to see the total amount of money I need to have available in the checking account. Here is an example.

	A	B	C	D	E	F	G	H		
1		Your Church								
2		Net Payroll								
3		Biweekly								
4										
5	Date						6.20%	1.45%		
6	Employee	Hourly Rate or Salary $	# of Hours	Gross Pay	Federal W/H	State W/H	Employee FICA	Employee Medicare	Additional Medicare	Net Pay
7	Susan Administrator	$ 1,050.00		$1,050.00	83		$ 65.10	$ 15.23		$ 886.68
8	Jack Janitor	$ 8.00	50	$ 400.00	17		$ 24.80	$ 5.80		$ 352.40
9										$ -
10										$ -
11								$ -		$ -
12										$ -
13	Total			$1,450.00	$ 100.00	$	$ 89.90	$ 21.03	$ -	$1,239.08
14										
15	Employer Portion due						$ 89.90	$ 21.03		
16										
17	Total Taxes due to IRS				$ 100.00		$ 179.80	$ 42.05	$ -	$ 321.85
18	Total Taxes due to State					$ -				-
19										
20	Total Cash Required for Payroll									$1,560.93

2014 rates.

Paycheck amounts.

The formulas in the spreadsheet check to see if there are hours included, in which case, the gross pay is calculated based on the number of hours times the rate. If no hours are included, it assumes the rate is a salary.

Federal and state withholding can be manually input from the Circular E tables. If you are experienced with spreadsheet calculations, you can link it to another spreadsheet with the percentage tax rate calculation.

The spreadsheet is setup with formulas for the SS and Medicare tax rates, so if they change next year, I only have to adjust those percentages, and the spreadsheet will calculate the new rates.

The net pay column subtracts the withholding (which you need to calculate from the IRS Circular E), SS, and Medicare taxes from the gross pay to compute the net pay. This is the amount of the paycheck due to the employee.

Additionally, I want the spreadsheet to tell me how much I need to send to the government. It calculates the employer match and then adds it to the employee withholding. These are added together with the federal withholding to calculate a total due to the IRS and state.

The Total Cash Required line is the total amount needed in the checking account for payroll. This spreadsheet is available as a download at www.accountantbesideyou.com or you can use this example to design your own.

F.   Posting the Payroll Expense

Once the checks are cut, you need to post this to your accounting system. For a spreadsheet system, input the gross wages in the wages expense item, the employer taxes in a payroll tax expense item. Cash will be reduced for the amount of the net pay and the payments to the government whether EFTPS or by check.

If you are using a computerized accounting program, you can post it as a journal entry. In this example, the gross payroll was $1450, and the employer tax expense was $110.93. Check 1010 was issued for one employee's net pay of $886.68, and check 1011 was issued for the second employee's net pay of $352.40. The federal income, Social Security, and Medicare taxes withheld plus the employer's tax totaled $321.85 and was electronically transferred to the US Treasury.

25	Account	Program	Debit	Credit
26	Payroll Expense	Admin	1,450.00	
27	Payroll Tax Expense	Admin	110.93	
28	Cash-ck 1010			886.68
29	Cash-ck 1011			352.40
30	Cash-EFTPS			321.85
31	Totals		1,560.93	1,560.93

The reductions in cash are broken out by checks and the electronic payments to make reconciling the bank account easier.

G.   Other Taxes

1.   FUTA & SUTA—Unemployment taxes

Churches are exempt from federal unemployment taxes but not necessarily from state unemployment taxes. Consult your state agency to see if your state grants exemptions to churches and if there are any filing requirements associated with it.

2.   Workers' Compensation

Most states require churches to provide Workers' Compensation Insurance. It is usually purchased through a company, not through the payroll system, but is based on your level of payroll. Again, you will need to check with your specific state for requirements.

3.   Temporary Disability Insurance Program

If you live in California, Hawaii, New Jersey, New York, Rhode Island, or Puerto Rico, contact your state's appropriate agency to see if this applies.

H.   Payroll Tax Deposits

Once your employees have been paid, you need to remit the money withheld and the employer match to the federal government. For most churches, this needs to be done monthly. Late payments may incur penalties. We'll now look at when and how to pay these deposits.

1.   Tax Deposit Schedule

The frequency of your payroll deposits is determined by the tax liability due.

If your tax liability is expected to be less than $1000 annually, you can call the IRS at 1-800-829-4933 before April 1st of the year and request permission to file a Form 944. Once you have written notification from the IRS, you will only need to file and pay annually. The filing and the payment is due by January 31st of the following year.

If you have less than $50,000 of tax deposits due per quarter in the past, you will need to file monthly. The payments must be made by the 15th day of the following month for the last month's payroll.

If your payroll tax deposits are greater than $50,000, you will follow the semiweekly deposit schedule. If the payday falls on a Wednesday, Thursday, or Friday, deposit the taxes by the following Wednesday. If the payday is any other day of the week, deposit the taxes by the following Friday.

2. EFTPS—Electronic Federal Tax Payment System

The federal government is requiring all federal tax deposits to be made using electronic funds. The Electronic Federal Tax Payment System (EFTPS) is a free service provided by the Department of Treasury. The website for EFTPS is www.eftps.gov and the telephone number is 1-800-555-4477.

If you are just receiving your EIN, you will be pre-enrolled in EFTPS and should receive information on activating the assigned PIN (personal identification number). Once you have enrolled and have an activated PIN, you can submit your federal deposits directly from your bank to the government.

Login

In order to make, view or cancel a Payment, you must first login.

Please enter your Employer Identification Number (EIN) or your Social Security Number (SSN), PIN, and Internet password in the fields below. If you do not have a PIN, please enroll first.

EIN (for Business)   [ ] - [ ]

or

SSN (for Individual)   [ ] - [ ] - [ ]

PIN   [ ]

Internet Password   [ ]

Need a Password

CANCEL   LOGIN ▶

Once you are logged in, it will take you step by step through how to input your bank account and routing number. Payments can be scheduled in advance, so even if you are not working on the due date, the payment can be made on time.

I.   Payroll Tax Filings

Just because you have deposited the withholding and taxes, don't think you are finished yet. Unless you are a very small filer and been told by the IRS to file an annual Form 944, you will need to prepare a Form 941-Employer's Quarterly Tax Return.

The 941 reconciles the monthly payments you made to the total liability for the quarter. It is due the last day of the month following the end of the quarter (i.e. April 30, July 31, October 31, and January 31). It reports to the IRS the number of employees, total wages paid during the quarter, and withholdings and total payroll taxes paid.

> *Form 941 may be filed electronically or mailed. If you are using an accounting software package, see if there is an efile option.*

On the IRS website is a fileable version of the form: http://www.irs.gov/pub/irs-pdf/f941.pdf. In the following pages, I'm including screens shots of the form so you can see what is required. To get started, you will need the last quarter's payroll information.

1.   941 Line by line instructions

The top section is for your EIN, legal name of the church, and address. To the right, you will notice a box listing the months. Mark the months you will be reporting on.

Part 1 Line 1: Enter the number of employees you had receiving wages during the quarter.

Line #2: Enter the taxable wages paid to employees. (Do not include the minister's housing allowance—see next chapter)

Line #3: Enter the amount of federal *income* tax withheld from employees' checks for the quarter.

Line #4: Check this box only if **no** wages or compensations were subject to Social Security and Medicare **such as a qualifying minister**. (*If you checked this box, you can skip down to line 6.*)

Line #5a: Enter the amount of taxable wages paid to non-minister employees. (*Do not include any amounts paid to qualifying ministers.*)

Line #5a: Column 2: Multiply line 5a by percentage shown.

Line #5b: Does not apply to churches.

Line #5c: Enter the amount of taxable wages paid to non-minister employees. (*Do not include any amounts paid to qualifying ministers.*)

Line #5c: Column 2: Multiply line 5a by percentage shown.

Line #5d: Only needed for employees paid over $200,000.

Line #5e: Total Social Security and Medicare taxes due.

Line #5f: Skip

Line #6: Add lines 3 and 5e.

Line #7 thru 9: Churches will not usually need to use these lines.

Line #10: Add lines 6 thru 9. Usually will just be the amount on 6.

Line #11: Total deposits for the quarter. (This is for medium category churches with a payroll tax liability over $2500 per quarter that have been making monthly deposits.)

Line #12: If line 10 is more than line 11, enter the difference. Hopefully, this is 0.

Line #13: If line 11 is more than line 10, enter the overpayment and select if you will be applying it to the next return or if you would like a refund sent.

The second page requires you to type in the church name and EIN at the top.

Part 2 Line 14: Explains to the IRS the frequency of your deposits. Select the first option only if you consistently have deposits due of less than $2500 per quarter. If you have been depositing on a monthly basis, even if less than $2500 per quarter, you need to select the second box and enter your monthly deposit amounts. The totals MUST equal Line 10 on the first page. If your church was large enough to be depositing semiweekly, select the third box instead and complete a Schedule B (available on the IRS website).

Part 3: Is usually unnecessary.

Part 4: Allows you to have someone else discuss the tax return with the IRS. This could be your outside accountant or a church member who is helping out. It is not required.

Part 5: Must be signed by an official of the church. The bookkeeper is NOT an allowed signer per the IRS. The minister, treasurer, and president of the council are all options.

Form **941 for 2014:** Employer's QUARTERLY Federal Tax Return
(Rev. January 2014)   Department of the Treasury — Internal Revenue Service

950114

OMB No. 1545-0029

Employer identification number (EIN)

Name (not your trade name)

Trade name (if any)

Address

Number   Street   Suite or room number

City   State   ZIP code

Foreign country name   Foreign province/county   Foreign postal code

Report for this Quarter of 2014
(Check one.)

1: January, February, March

2: April, May, June

3: July, August, September

4: October, November, December

Instructions and prior year forms are available at www.irs.gov/form941.

Read the separate instructions before you complete Form 941. Type or print within the boxes.

Part 1:   Answer these questions for this quarter.

1	Number of employees who received wages, tips, or other compensation for the pay period including: *Mar. 12* (Quarter 1), *June 12* (Quarter 2), *Sept. 12* (Quarter 3), or *Dec. 12* (Quarter 4)	1
2	Wages, tips, and other compensation	2
3	Federal income tax withheld from wages, tips, and other compensation	3
4	If no wages, tips, and other compensation are subject to social security or Medicare tax	☐ Check and go to line 6.

		Column 1	Column 2
5a	Taxable social security wages		$\times .124 =$
5b	Taxable social security tips		$\times .124 =$
5c	Taxable Medicare wages & tips		$\times .029 =$
5d	Taxable wages & tips subject to Additional Medicare Tax withholding		$\times .009 =$

5e	Add Column 2 from lines 5a, 5b, 5c, and 5d	5e
5f	Section 3121(q) Notice and Demand—Tax due on unreported tips (see instructions)	5f
6	Total taxes before adjustments. Add lines 3, 5e, and 5f	6
7	Current quarter's adjustment for fractions of cents	7
8	Current quarter's adjustment for sick pay	8
9	Current quarter's adjustments for tips and group-term life insurance	9
10	Total taxes after adjustments. Combine lines 6 through 9	10
11	Total deposits for this quarter, including overpayment applied from a prior quarter and overpayments applied from Form 941-X, 941-X (PR), 944-X, 944-X (PR), or 944-X (SP) filed in the current quarter	11
12	Balance due. If line 10 is more than line 11, enter the difference and see instructions	12
13	Overpayment. If line 11 is more than line 10, enter the difference [ ] Check one: ☐ Apply to next return. ☐ Send a refund.	

▶ You MUST complete both pages of Form 941 and SIGN it.   Next ▶

For Privacy Act and Paperwork Reduction Act Notice, see the back of the Payment Voucher.   Cat. No. 17001Z   Form **941** (Rev. 1-2014)

The form also includes a voucher to use only if your total taxes for the preceding quarter were less than $2500.

If not submitted electronically, the form must be mailed by the due date to the address listed in the instructions. The address is dependent on which state your church is located in.

950214

Name *(not your trade name)*	Employer identification number (EIN)

Part 2: Tell us about your deposit schedule and tax liability for this quarter.

If you are unsure about whether you are a monthly schedule depositor or a semiweekly schedule depositor, see Pub. 15 (Circular E), section 11.

14 Check one: ☐ Line 10 on this return is less than $2,500 or line 10 on the return for the prior quarter was less than $2,500, and you did not incur a $100,000 next-day deposit obligation during the current quarter. If line 10 for the prior quarter was less than $2,500 but line 10 on this return is $100,000 or more, you must provide a record of your federal tax liability. If you are a monthly schedule depositor, complete the deposit schedule below; if you are a semiweekly schedule depositor, attach Schedule B (Form 941). Go to Part 3.

☐ **You were a monthly schedule depositor for the entire quarter.** Enter your tax liability for each month and total liability for the quarter, then go to Part 3.

Tax liability: Month 1 [   ] .

Month 2 [   ] .

Month 3 [   ] .

Total liability for quarter [   ] .   Total must equal line 10.

☐ **You were a semiweekly schedule depositor for any part of this quarter.** Complete Schedule B (Form 941), Report of Tax Liability for Semiweekly Schedule Depositors, and attach it to Form 941.

Part 3: Tell us about your business. If a question does NOT apply to your business, leave it blank.

15 If your business has closed or you stopped paying wages . . . . ☐ Check here, and

enter the final date you paid wages [/   /   ]

16 If you are a seasonal employer and you do not have to file a return for every quarter of the year . . ☐ Check here.

Part 4: May we speak with your third-party designee?

Do you want to allow an employee, a paid tax preparer, or another person to discuss this return with the IRS? See the instructions for details.

☐ Yes. Designee's name and phone number [   ] [   ]

Select a 5-digit Personal Identification Number (PIN) to use when talking to the IRS. [ ][ ][ ][ ][ ]

☐ No.

Part 5: Sign here. You MUST complete both pages of Form 941 and SIGN it.

Under penalties of perjury, I declare that I have examined this return, including accompanying schedules and statements, and to the best of my knowledge and belief, it is true, correct, and complete. Declaration of preparer (other than taxpayer) is based on all information of which preparer has any knowledge.

X Sign your name here [   ]

Print your name here [   ]

Print your title here [   ]

Date [/   /   ]

Best daytime phone [   ]

Paid Preparer Use Only   Check if you are self-employed . . . ☐

Preparer's name	[ ]	PTIN	[ ]
Preparer's signature	[ ]	Date	[/ /]
Firm's name (or yours if self-employed)	[ ]	EIN	[ ]
Address	[ ]	Phone	[ ]
City	[ ] State [ ]	ZIP code	[ ]

Page 2   Form **941** (Rev. 1-2014)

2.   State Filings

Don't forget most states have their own payroll tax forms and filing deadlines. Most are due the same month as the 941, but you will need to verify it with your state department of revenue. For your convenience, I have added a page on accountantbesideyou.com with links to each of the states' Departments of Revenue and Secretaries of State.

J.   Year End Filings

1.   W-2 and W-3

After the calendar year end, your employees need to know the total amount of wages received and how much was taken out for taxes in the previous year. The W-2 gives them this information and is also sent to the federal government.

A W-2 has at least three copies. The first (Copy A) is in red and is sent to the Social Security Administration with a transmittal form (W-3). Copy B in black is to be filed with the employee's federal return. Copy C is included for the employee's records. There is a Copy 1 (and 2, if needed) for the state, city, or local department of revenue.

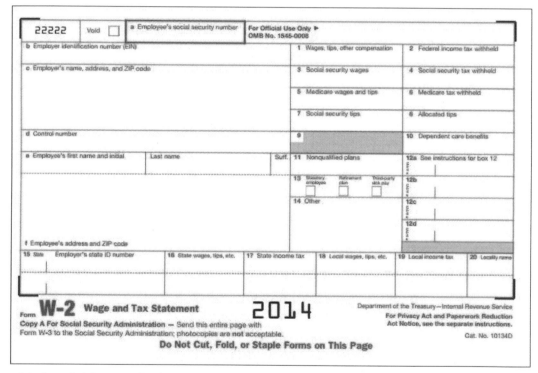

This is a fairly simple form to complete. At the very top, enter your employee's SSN in box a. Box b is the church's EIN, followed by the church's legal name and address in box c. The Control number in box d is for your use if you are numbering the W-2 for tracking purposes. It can be left blank. Box e and f are for the employee's name and address.

Let's step through the numbered boxes next.

Box 1: Total wages and compensation paid to the employee. This is before any deductions.

Keep in mind this box is asking for wages paid, not earned. If you paid your employees on January 2 for the previous two weeks of work, you would not include it.

It should include any other taxable compensation, such as travel advances—not per diems—for which receipts were not received as discussed in Chapter IX.

Box 2: Federal income tax withheld. This is the total amount of federal taxes withheld from the employee for the year.

Box 3: Social Security wages for non-ministers are usually the same as total wages. Differences may occur if the employee was paid more than the $117,000 base or other compensation was included. As will be discussed in the next chapter, ministers do not have Social Security or Medicare withheld.

Box 4: Tax withheld on the Social Security wages. This should equal 6.2% of box 3.

Box 5: For non-ministers, Medicare wages and tips will usually be the same as box 1, unless there is other compensation included.

Box 6: Tax withheld on the amount in box 5. This amount should equal 1.45% of box 5.

Boxes 7-9: These are not-commonly used by churches.

Boxes 10-14: These relate to dependent care benefits, retirement plans, and other miscellaneous items too detailed for the scope of this book. Your accountant or retirement benefits administrator will need to give you specific directions for your organization.

Boxes 15-20: This is where you input the church's state and/or local identification number and the state and local income and taxes withheld for the employee.

Once all of the employee's information is entered, double check the SSN and address and total each of the boxes of all of the W-2s. This information will be entered into the W-3 Transmittal of Wage and Tax Statement.

Before you start entering data in the W-3, pull out the four quarterly reports (941s) and double check that the four of them total to the same amount as the totals of your W-2s. For example, the four quarters of Total Taxable Wages must equal the amount in Box 1. The four quarters of Federal Income Tax Withheld must equal box 2, etc. Investigate any discrepancies and make the appropriate adjustments.

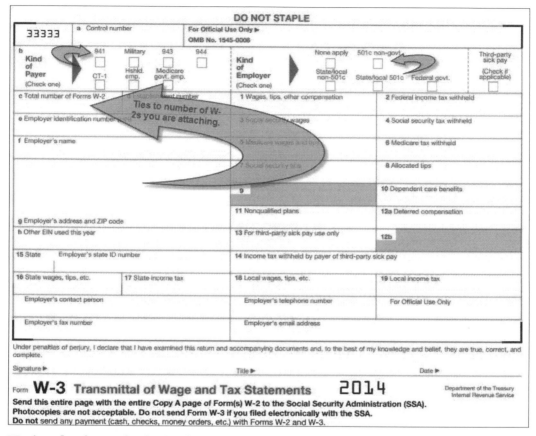

Notice the forms look similar to the W-2. Starting at the top, you will need to mark the kind of payer you are. Unless you are small enough to be a 944 filer (discussed earlier in the chapter), you will select 941. The Kind of Employer option for a church is 501c non-govt.

Box c asks for the total number of forms you are submitting with the transmittal statement. Box d allows for an establishment number in case you have several locations using the same EIN.

The other lettered boxes request your legal name, address, federal and state EINs, etc. The numbered boxes are the totals of that box from all of the attached W-2s. Once you are sure your totals reconcile with the four 941s, complete the form, sign, title, and date. Include (but do NOT staple) the red Copy A for each W-2 and mail to the address listed in the instructions on the form. These are typically due by the last day of February.

You cannot download a usable W-2 and W-3 from the web!

The original that's filed with the IRS is printed in red ink and is read by a scanner.

You can order forms from the IRS at no charge or purchase them from an office supply store. You can reach the IRS at 1-800-TAX-FORM to request the ones you need or order them online at irs.gov.

Order your W-2 and W-3 forms from the IRS as early as possible. If you wait until January, you may not get them in time, and office supply stores may run short as well.

K.   Summary

I know this chapter was rather complex. But you now have the tools and ability to calculate and pay the normal payroll, which can save your church a lot of money.

The amount of an employee's payroll check is determined by calculating the federal tax withholding using either the tax table method or the percentage method, taking into account the number of allowances he has requested. If your state has an income tax, you will calculate that withholding based on the state charts. Next, calculate Social Security and Medicare withholding. From the gross wages subtract the total of the withholdings. This will give you the net payroll check amount.

The taxes withheld and the employer taxes must be deposited with the US Treasury and quarterly reports filed (unless you have been given approval for an annual filing). The taxes are filed electronically, so the church needs to set up an account through the IRS. After year end, the employees need to receive a W-2 showing annual earnings and taxes withheld. These are filed with a transmittal form W-3 to the government.

You have gone through the steps of calculating withholding, preparing the payroll checks, recording the entry, making the tax deposit, and filing the required forms for a normal payroll. Next, we'll go over what is not normal about church payroll—ministers.

XII.   Payroll — Part III: Ministers and the IRS

We all know ministers are special people. Even the IRS thinks so as ministers are accorded some unique tax situations.

1. Ministers are considered employees under common law rules, but payments for services are considered self-employment income. I assume this is due to the degree of control factor the IRS tests for and has been established in numerous tax court cases. For a church, this means no Social Security or Medicare taxes are withheld or matched. For the minister, it means he must file and pay his Social Security and Medicare taxes quarterly as if he were self-employed.

2. A minister may be considered an independent contractor, which will determine how his expenses are classified on his tax return.

3. Ministers are also allowed a parsonage or house allowance, which is exempt from income tax but subject to self-employment taxes (SS & Medicare). This can be a substantial federal income tax savings for the minister.

4. If the minister is a member of an exempt religious order and has taken a vow of poverty, his earnings may be exempt from the income and self-employment taxes.

5. For other than retired ministers, a gift given to a minister may be treated as compensation for services and included in gross income. This includes love offerings.

6. The IRS understands ministers often have non-reimbursed expenses in the course of doing business for the church, and there are specific rules on how to handle them.

In this chapter, I'll explain each of these in detail and show you how to handle the resolutions required, payments to the ministers, and the necessary filings.

A.   Who is a Minister (for Tax Purposes)

To define who the Internal Revenue Code considers a minister, I will quote from the IRS.gov websites, *Minister Audit Technique Guide*.

To qualify for the special tax provisions available to ministers, an individual must be a "minister" and must perform services "in the exercise of his ministry." Treas. Reg. § 1.107-1(a) incorporates the rules of Treas. Reg. § 1.1402(c)-5 in determining whether the individual is performing the duties of a "minister of the gospel."

Treas. Reg. § 1.1402(c)-5 requires that an individual be a "duly ordained, commissioned, or licensed minister of a church." The Tax Court has interpreted this phrase to be disjunctive, finding the purpose is not to limit benefits to the ordained, but is to prevent self-appointed ministers from benefiting.

Services performed by a minister in the exercise of the ministry include:

1. Ministration of sacerdotal functions,

2. Conduct of religious worship,

3. Control, conduct, and maintenance of religious organizations (including the religious boards, societies, and other integral agencies of such organizations), under the authority of a religious body constituting a church or denomination.

> *In a nutshell, if the pastor is licensed or ordained, administers the sacraments of the church (i.e. weddings, funerals, baptisms, and communion), is considered a religious leader by the church, conducts the worship, and has management responsibilities in the church, he is entitled to treatment as a clergy for tax purposes.*

But note, he must be all of the above. Youth ministers, deacons, and non-ordained persons are not considered a minister for tax purposes. If your church has more than one ordained minister who seems to fit this criteria, you will want to consult a tax specialist to see which can legally be considered a minister for tax purposes.

B.   Employee or Independent Contractor

As the IRS has the minister pay his own self-employment taxes, you may wonder why it matters whether he is an employee or an independent contractor. The main difference, besides whether the church issues a W-2 or a 1099, is how the minister handles his business expenses. For an independent contractor, business expenses are reported on the Schedule C. If the minister is considered an employee, the expenses are subject to statutory limitations as an employee business expense in his itemized deductions.

The employee vs independent contractor issue is highly scrutinized by the IRS in most industries. There are three categories the IRS considers to determine the status of the person: behavioral control, financial control, and the relationship of the parties.

- Behavioral control is related to the amount of control the person has to direct how the work is performed.

- Financial control looks at whether the worker can realize profit or loss, has significant investment, and un-reimbursed expenses.

- The relationship of the parties reflects the intent regarding the control. That is a legalistic way of saying the person hiring him intends to oversee him like an employee or intends to let him have more autonomy and treat him as a contractor.

Most pastors should be considered employees. They typically have a governing council they work with or for to determine the work to be performed. The church probably pays for their office or, at least, a computer to do their work, and reimburses the expenses they can afford.

Exceptions to this would be supply pastors or missionaries who travel from church to church, filling in or working for short periods. Another potential exception would be a minister in a new church who is using his own funds to get everything up and running. He may be considered an independent contractor until the church has a council and regular offices.

> *Bottom line is, you will play it safer by treating your minister as an employee and issuing a W-2 at year end.*

C.   Housing or Parsonage Allowance

The housing allowance is a wonderful benefit for ministers. It allows them to receive the cost of housing free from federal income tax. It is NOT exempt from self-employment taxes. We'll go over the necessary qualifications and requirements.

1.   Qualifications

In order to qualify for the exclusion from federal income tax, two very important conditions must be satisfied:

1. The housing allowance must be board approved before it was paid—a housing allowance is NEVER retroactive, and

2. The minister must actually spend the allowance on eligible housing expenses during the year.

Your church must make sure the amount of the allowance for housing is determined before it is paid. It should be included in a board-approved resolution and properly documented in the church records annually.

2.   Other requirements

The exclusion only applies if the church designates the amount of the parsonage allowance in advance of the tax year. Your church does not have control over the second condition mentioned above but should use the minister's information to determine the allowance. The minister has the responsibility of tracking actual housing expenses.

The fair rental value of the parsonage or the parsonage allowance cannot be more than reasonable pay for the ministerial services performed. This means if a reasonable salary for ministers in your area is $50,000 annually, you cannot give the minister a $75,000 housing allowance.

Unless your minister has outside sources of income, I strongly discourage you from allowing his entire salary to be considered housing allowance. The IRS may question how he is surviving on only a housing allowance.

The amount of the allowance the minister can exclude from his gross income is the LEAST of:

1.   the amount actually used to provide a home,

2.   the amount officially designated as a housing allowance, or

3.   the fair rental value (FRV) of the home, including furnishings and appurtenances such as a garage plus the cost of utilities. IRS∫107(2).

Let's review what that means for the various housing situations a minister may have.

3.   Church-owned parsonage

If the church owns a parsonage and pays the utilities and taxes, the minister and the council need to agree on a fair rental value (FRV). This can be determined by comparing the local rental market's similar properties. If you have a real estate agent in your congregation, they should have access to the data you need. Be sure to document your assumptions for the FRV.

If the FRV comparisons do not include utilities, add the average monthly utility bill for the parsonage to the FRV for the housing allowance. For this example, let's assume the FRV is $800 and utilities average $200 per month and are paid by the church, for a total of $12,000 annually. The minister receives an annual salary of $40,000 along with the use of the parsonage.

His gross income for federal income tax purposes would be $40,000, but he will need to pay self-employment tax on income of $52,000 ($40,000+$12,000 FRV+utilities).

4. Minister-owned housing

The next minister owns his own house. He has mortgage payments of $20,000 per year, utilities of $5000 annually, and $4000 of home maintenance and furnishing. His church had authorized a $35,000 housing allowance. The fair rental value of his home, as furnished, is $25,000 per year.

Recall the minister is only allowed to exclude the LEAST of the actual cost to provide a home, the officially designated housing allowance, or the FRV including utilities. Therefore, we'll need to examine the three amounts:

1. Actual expenses equal $29,000,
2. Designated housing allowances equals $35,000
3. and the FRV including utilities equals $30,000 ($25,000+$5000)

The least of these costs is his actual cost of $29,000. He may exclude $29,000 of the $35,000 housing allowance he received from federal income taxes, but must add the remaining $6000 to his gross income. The entire $35,000 of housing allowance is included in the calculation of his self-employment tax.

Ministers cannot deduct actual expenses greater than the designated housing allowance or the FRV including utilities.

5. Other situations

Once a mortgage is paid off, the minister's actual expenses may be dramatically below the FRV. In the court case, Swaggart v. Commissioner, T.C. Memo. 1984-409, it was ruled the minister must still take into account the FRV. Without the mortgage, the actual expenses were the least of the three criteria (actual expenses, designated housing allowance or FRV) and must be used to determine the exclusion.

If a minister takes out a home equity loan for a personal reason, i.e. children's college tuition or new car, the payments cannot be used in calculating actual expenses. This is because the money was not used to "provide a home." The interest on the home equity loan can be deducted as an itemized deduction (subject to limitations).

If a home equity loan was taken out to replace the roof or add a garage, this could be considered "providing a home" and therefore included in the calculation of the exemption.

If the minister owns a shared house (a duplex or a house with an apartment to rent), any improvements and expenses must be allocated between the income-producing portion and the living portion. He can deduct the portion of the expenses relating to the income-producing property from the rental income, but he cannot include it in the calculations of his actual cost for housing.

If a church pays for the minister's personal mortgage directly to the mortgage company, the value must be included in gross income on his W-2. It is preferable for the minister's tax situation to set up a housing allowance and pay the minister instead.

The church should not reimburse the minister for **actual** housing expenses, like the electric bills or plumber's charges. These cannot be accurately known in advance, and the rules require the amount of the housing allowance be designated before the beginning of the tax year for it to be exempt.

> *Remember, any housing allowance MUST be documented in the church records before the beginning of the tax year.*

6.   Example Parsonage Allowance Resolution

On Vickey's freechurchaccounting.com website, she offers an example of the minutes required for a housing allowance resolution. You will not use all of the paragraphs listed here. Delete the paragraphs not needed for your situation.

Parsonage Allowance Resolution

It was discussed that under the tax law a minister of the gospel is not subject to federal income tax on the "housing allowance paid to him as part of his compensation to the extent used by him to rent or provide a home."

The parsonage owned by the church has a rental value of $_____ and is provided for the convenience of the church. Actual utility expenses will be paid by the church, and they will amount to approximately $_____ for the year.

After considering the statement "Pastor's Estimate of Home Expenses" prepared by _____, a motion was made and seconded and passed to adopt the following resolution:

Resolved that Pastor _____ is to receive a total cash remuneration of $_____(salary) for the year 20____. Of this amount, $_____ (housing expenses paid from salary) is hereby designated as housing allowance.

Resolved that as long as Pastor _____ is our employee, the above amount of housing/parsonage allowance shall apply to all future years until modified.

Date_____ Signed_____

7.   Allowed expenses for the parsonage allowance

Only the amount the minister actually spends on the home can be considered exempt from federal income tax. If the minister has a $20,000 parsonage allowance, but only $15,000 of allowed expenses, the remaining $5000 must be included in his gross income for tax purposes. Allowed expenses are any expense relating to renting a home, purchasing a home, and/or maintaining a home.

The church does not have to assure the minister spent the full amount of the allowance. It is the minister's repsonsibility to fill out his tax return correctly.

Some of the eligible expenses relating to renting or purchasing a home include:

- Down payment on a home
- Home mortgage payments, including both interest and principal
- Real estate taxes
- Personal property tax
- Fire and homeowners liability insurance
- Rental payments
- Cost of acquiring a home (i.e. legal fees, bank fees, title fees, etc.)

The housing allowance can also be used for maintaining a home. Some of the eligible costs or expenses include:

- Home improvements
- Minor repairs
- Utilities
- Furnishings and appliances (dishwasher, TV, refrigerator, pool table, vacuum cleaner, personal computer, etc.)
- Home decor (rugs, curtains, plants, knick knacks, wallpaper, paint, towels, bedding, etc.)
- Lawn care (lawnmower, garden hose, sod, landscape tools, etc.)
- Basic telephone services
- Cable TV
- Internet service
- Miscellaneous (light bulbs, cleaning supplies, etc.)

Examples of expenses which are **not** eligible are:

- Foods
- Servants
- Cleaning service or expenses for a person to clean your house
- Groceries
- Personal toiletries
- CDs and DVDs
- Personal computer software

8. Example of a Pastor's Estimate of Home Expenses Worksheet

Once again, I refer to Vickey's work in designing a worksheet for your pastor to determine his home expenses. The completed worksheet can be reviewed by the council before the beginning of the tax year to determine the appropriate level of parsonage allowance.

Pastor's Estimate of Home Expenses

Name of church _____

Position held _____

Housing allowance for the coming year of 20____. I expect to incur the following expenses to rent or otherwise provide a home.

Rent or payments on purchase of a house including down payment, principal payments, interest, taxes, and improvements:

$_____

Furnishings and appliances:

$_____

Utilities :

$_____

Other housing expenses (cleaning supplies, etc.):

$_____

Miscellaneous repairs:

$_____

Total: $_____

Signature_____ Date_____

---

9. Retired ministers' housing

Parsonage allowances can also be given to retired ministers. A retired minister may receive it as part of his pension benefits. The trustees of the retirement plan may designate an amount using the "least of" rules. The entire amount received is excludable from net earnings from self-employment even if a portion is not excludable for income tax purposes.

D. Income to be Reported by a Minister

Besides his salary, the pastor may receive special gifts for services. This could be fees received directly from individuals for performing wedding, funeral, or baptismal services. These should be added to his gross income for self-employment and income tax purposes, along with any expense allowances received under a non-accountable plan (as discussed in Chapter IX). If the fees are paid to the church and not the minister directly, they do not need to be added to the minister's gross income.

Members of the congregation may also give the pastor gifts of cash or property. This is known as a *love offering*. Whether this is taxable or not depends on the intention. For example, when members of a certain congregation thought they might lose their pastor because of his low pay, several got together and gave the pastor a generous cash "gift." The courts ruled this was taxable to the pastor as it was in anticipation of the services he would be providing.

You may recall I began the book with the story of a pastor who received large amounts of love offerings but did not report them as income. The amounts were significant and became one of the determining factors in sentencing him to jail.

If a congregation passes around a collection for a retiring minister, this could be considered a gift and not compensation for past services.

> *To play it safe, if a significant gift is being offered to your minister, check with your local CPA or tax advisor to understand the tax consequences.*

E.   Minister's Business Expenses

Understanding that a minister may have unreimbursed business expenses, the tax code allows ministers who are categorized as employees the ability to deduct unreimbursed employee business expense, non-accountable reimbursed business expenses, plus miscellaneous itemized deductions up to a two percent floor. The term "two percent floor" means if all the business plus miscellaneous itemized expenses you wish to deduct are less than 2% of your adjusted gross income, you cannot deduct them. If they total more than the 2%, you can deduct the amount greater than 2%.

For example, if the minister has a salary of $30,000, his two percent floor is $600. If his unreimbursed employee business expenses plus miscellaneous itemized deductions were $750, he can only deduct $150. If they were $500, he would have no deduction allowed.

If the church adopts an accountable reimbursement plan as discussed in Chapter IX, the limitations on deductibility may be avoided. Reimbursements made under the accountable plan are excluded from the gross income and not reported on his W-2.

If the minister is given an expense allowance but is not required to show documentation nor return any unused funds, it does not meet the reimbursement requirement and is therefore included as taxable income.

F.   Exemption for Self-Employment Tax

Pastors must pay the Social Security and Medicare taxes with a few exceptions.

- The minister is of a religious order whose members have taken a vow of poverty.

- The minister is subject only to the social security laws of a foreign country.

- Or the minister has requested **and the IRS has approved** an exemption based on conscientious opposition.

In order to claim the exemption based on conscientious opposition, the ordained minister must be conscientiously opposed to receiving public insurance due to religious beliefs, not simply opposed to paying for public insurance. He must file Form 4361 requesting the exemption and establish that the organization that ordained him is a tax-exempt religious organization and the organization is a church or a convention of churches.

Form 4361 must be filed by the due date of the minister's income tax Form 1040 after the second tax year in which at least $400 in self-employment ministerial earnings were received.

If the minister receives the Social Security and Medicare tax exemption, it is only valid for the revenue he receives as services performed by a minister. It does not apply to other self-employment income.

G.   Tax Filings for Ministers

1.   Church's filings

For ministers treated as employees, they will be paid with the other employees. The church will not withhold federal taxes unless the pastor has voluntarily requested it. Check with your state's department of revenue to verify their withholding requirements. There is a list of the state's Department of Revenue in the appendix, as well as live links on accountantbesideyou.com.

The church should NOT withhold any money for Social Security or Medicare, nor should it submit any related employer tax. The minister's income will be included in the church's total on the quarterly 941s. The housing allowance amount is not filed with the quarterly reports.

At year end, the W-2 for the minister will include his salary without the housing allowance. The Social Security and Medicare wages will be recorded as $0. The housing allowance can be listed in Box 14 Other if desired, but it is not required.

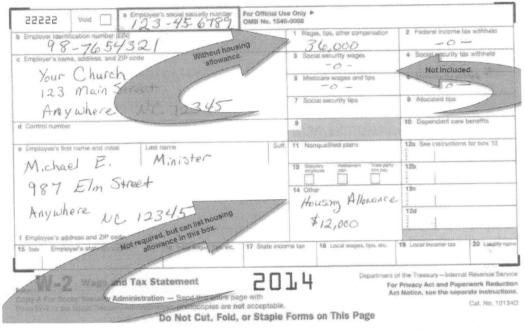

If the minister was treated as an independent contractor, he will receive a 1099 instead (see Chapter IX). The 1099 should not include the housing allowance. It is the minister's responsibility to report it.

2. Minister's filings

With the dual status, the minister is considered self-employed and must pay his self-employment taxes quarterly. There are penalties for not paying or underpaying the self-employment (and income taxes, if an independent contractor).

The quarterly taxes are filed with Form 1040-ES, Estimated Tax for Individuals. The instructions for the form, available at http://www.irs.gov/pub/irs-pdf/f1040es.pdf, include the following worksheet to help with the tax and deduction calculation.

**2014 Self-Employment Tax and Deduction Worksheet for
Lines 1 and 11 of the Estimated Tax Worksheet**

Keep for Your Records

1a. Enter your expected income and profits subject to self-employment tax* .... 1a. _____

  b. If you will have farm income and also receive social security retirement or disability
     benefits, enter your expected Conservation Reserve Program payments that will be
     included on Schedule F (Form 1040) or listed on Schedule K-1 (Form 1065) ..... 1b. _____

2. Subtract line 1b from line 1a .... 2. _____

3. Multiply line 2 by 92.35% (.9235) .... 3. _____

4. Multiply line 3 by 2.9% (.029) .... 4. _____

5. Social security tax maximum income 5. $117,000

6. Enter your expected wages (if subject to social security tax or the 6.2% portion of
   tier 1 railroad retirement tax) .... 6. _____

7. Subtract line 6 from line 5 .... 7. _____

   Note. *If line 7 is zero or less, enter -0- on line 9 and skip to line 10.*

8. Enter the **smaller** of line 3 or line 7 .... 8. _____

9. Multiply line 8 by 12.4% (.124) .... 9. _____

10. Add lines 4 and 9. Enter the result here and on line 11 of your 2014 Estimated Tax Worksheet .... 10. _____

11. Multiply line 10 by 50% (.50). This is your expected deduction for self-employment
    tax on Form 1040, line 27. Subtract this amount when figuring your expected AGI on
    line 1 of your 2014 Estimated Tax Worksheet ....

* Your net profit from self-employment is found on Schedule C (Form 1040), line 31; Schedule F (Form 1040), line 34; Schedule K-1 (Form 1065), box 14, code A; and Schedule K-1 (Form 1065-B), box 9, code J1.

Include salary, housing allowance, and any advances or allowances not fully used.

Once the above worksheet is completed, you are ready to fill out the 2014 Estimated Tax Worksheet shown on the facing page. Follow the IRS instructions on filling out the worksheet on the following page to determine your tax liability. These worksheets are NOT sent to the IRS, but used by the tax payer to determine the amount due.

Any tax owed is submitted to the IRS with the Payment Voucher shown below.

Form **1040-ES**
Department of the Treasury
Internal Revenue Service

2014 Estimated Tax

Payment Voucher 4

OMB No. 1545-0074

File only if you are making a payment of estimated tax by check or money order. Mail this voucher with your check or money order payable to **"United States Treasury."** Write your social security number and "2014 Form 1040-ES" on your check or money order. Do not send cash. Enclose, but do not staple or attach, your payment with this voucher.

Calendar year—**Due Jan. 15, 2015**

Amount of estimated tax you are paying by check or money order.

| | Dollars | Cents |

Based on the tax worksheet

Your first name and initial	Your last name	Your social security number
If joint payment, complete for spouse		
Spouse's first name and initial	Spouse's last name	Spouse's social security number
Address (number, street, and apt. no.)		
City, state, and ZIP code. (If a foreign address, enter city, also complete spaces below.)		
Foreign country name	Foreign province/county	Foreign postal code

Print or type

For Privacy Act and Paperwork Reduction Act Notice, see instructions.

Form 1040-ES (2014)

2014 Estimated Tax Worksheet — *Keep for Your Records*

1	Adjusted gross income you expect in 2014 (see instructions)	1
2	• If you plan to itemize deductions, enter the estimated total of your itemized deductions. **Caution:** *If line 1 is over $152,525 your deduction may be reduced. See Pub. 505 for details.* • If you do not plan to itemize deductions, enter your standard deduction. }	2
3	Subtract line 2 from line 1	3
4	Exemptions. Multiply $3,950 by the number of personal exemptions. **Caution:** *See Worksheet 2-6 in Pub. 505 to figure the amount to enter if line 1 is over: $152,525*	4
5	Subtract line 4 from line 3	5
6	**Tax.** Figure your tax on the amount on line 5 by using the **2014 Tax Rate Schedules.** **Caution:** *If you will have qualified dividends or a net capital gain, or expect to exclude or deduct foreign earned income or housing, see Worksheets 2-7 and 2-8 in Pub. 505 to figure the tax.* . . .	6
7	Alternative minimum tax from **Form 6251** or included on **Form 1040A, line 28**	7
8	Add lines 6 and 7. Add to this amount any other taxes you expect to include in the total on Form 1040, line 44	8
9	Credits (see instructions). **Do not** include any income tax withholding on this line	9
10	Subtract line 9 from line 8. If zero or less, enter -0-	10
11	Self-employment tax (see instructions)	11
12	Other taxes (see instructions)	12
13a	Add lines 10 through 12	13a
b	Earned income credit, additional child tax credit, fuel tax credit, and refundable American opportunity credit	13b
c	**Total 2014 estimated tax.** Subtract line 13b from line 13a. If zero or less, enter -0- . . . ▶	13c
14a	Multiply line 13c by 90% (66²⁄₃% for farmers and fishermen)	14a	
b	Required annual payment based on prior year's tax (see instructions) .	14b	
c	**Required annual payment to avoid a penalty.** Enter the **smaller** of line 14a or 14b . . . ▶	14c
	Caution: *Generally, if you do not prepay (through income tax withholding and estimated tax payments) at least the amount on line 14c, you may owe a penalty for not paying enough estimated tax. To avoid a penalty, make sure your estimate on line 13c is as accurate as possible. Even if you pay the required annual payment, you may still owe tax when you file your return. If you prefer, you can pay the amount shown on line 13c. For details, see chapter 2 of Pub. 505.*	
15	Income tax withheld and estimated to be withheld during 2014 (including income tax withholding on pensions, annuities, certain deferred income, etc.)	15
16a	Subtract line 15 from line 14c	16a	
	Is the result zero or less? ☐ **Yes.** Stop here. You are not required to make estimated tax payments. ☐ **No.** Go to line 16b.	
b	Subtract line 15 from line 13c	16b	
	Is the result less than $1,000? ☐ **Yes.** Stop here. You are not required to make estimated tax payments. ☐ **No.** Go to line 17 to figure your required payment.	
17	If the first payment you are required to make is due April 15, 2014, enter ¼ of line 16a (minus any 2013 overpayment that you are applying to this installment) here, and on your estimated tax payment voucher(s) if you are paying by check or money order	17

As a self-employed individual, the minister can also file electronically through the EFTPS system discussed in Chapter XI. Go to the IRS website to sign up for electronic filing.

3. Year-end filings for ministers

Annually, the minister will use Schedule C or Schedule C-EZ to report his income or loss. This is the form where unreimbursed business expenses can be reported. Schedule C will be submitted with his 1040 (Federal Income Tax form). The first page of the Schedule C is shown here as an example.

Additionally, he is required to file Schedule SE (Form 1040) to report the Social Security and Medicare taxes. The instructions are at http://www.irs.gov/pub/irs-pdf/i1040sse.pdf and are fairly clear. The first page explains which schedule to use (Long or Short).

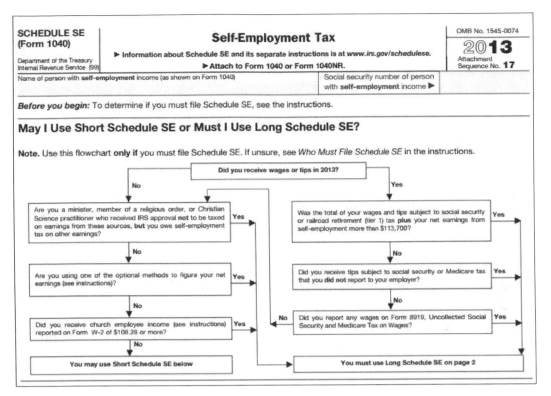

The bottom of the first page is the short form (not shown). The second page is the long form. Most ministers must use the Long Schedule SE.

> *This book is not intend to offer tax advice. If the church or the minister has any questions or issues, a local tax advisor should be consulted. Furthermore, as tax laws change frequently, the filer must familiarize himself with any new laws.*

H.   Designing a Minister Compensation Package

How a pastor's compensation package is designed and documented will make a significant difference on the tax effect to the pastor. A typical compensation package for a minister will have three main components: cash compensation, benefits, and reimbursement for job-related expenses. How the compensation is spread between these three categories will impact the amount of taxes the minister will pay.

Vickey has been noticing more churches harboring the misconception that they can pay for their pastor's "living expenses" tax free if they don't have a parsonage.

These churches don't have a housing allowance documented and sometimes even pay the pastor a check for everyday living expenses on top of his rent and utilities.

Without the housing allowance, the pastor must add these payments to his income and pay federal income tax on these expenses. The everyday living expenses payment is not proper and should be considered part of his taxable income.

If your church has this misconception, go back to Chapter XII and read the section on Housing Allowances to understand the rules and documentation required.

The *cash compensation* portion may include the minister's salary, housing/parsonage allowance, and Social Security/Medicare tax offset. Some congregations may also include an equity allowance for pastors living in parsonages to use upon retirement.

- The *minister's salary* is subject to federal, state, and local income taxes just like all employees. It is also used for calculating the retirement plan contributions.

- The *housing/parsonage allowance* (detailed in Chapter XII) allows some of the minister's compensation to be excluded from federal income taxes. Regardless of the amount designated as the allowance, the minister can only exclude the smallest of: the fair market value of rent plus utilities, actual costs of owning the house plus utilities, or the amount of the allowance. Therefore, the amount of the compensation package allocated to the housing allowance should be carefully calculated.

- A church does not withhold Social Security and Medicare taxes on a pastor nor pay the matching employer tax. A *Social Security-Medicare tax offset* is sometimes given to the pastor to offset 50% of the self-employment tax. This is subject to federal income tax and self-employment taxes.

- An *equity allowance* for pastors living in a parsonage allows a church to designate an amount for the minister to assist with housing after retirement. This is paid by the church into a fund which is not given to the minister until his retirement and is subject to federal income tax once the minister uses it. It is subjected to self-employment taxes when designated and possibly state and local income taxes. Be sure to review with a local tax specialist before establishing an equity allowance.

The rationale behind the equity allowance is that the ministers who live in parsonages their whole career do not have any equity built up in their home for retirement.

The *benefits* portion of the compensation package may include health insurance, life insurance, disability insurance, and retirement. Paid vacations, sick days, and sabbaticals are also common benefits for a minister. Because the cost is included in the minister's salary, it often is excluded from a dollar value in the package. But, as you are working with your pastor on determining the appropriate compensation, the amount of paid leave can be negotiated.

The *reimbursement* portion of the package details the types and limits of job-related expenses the church will reimburse the pastor for. If your church has a documented accountable plan, as discussed in Chapter IX, these reimbursements are not taxable to the pastor and do not need to be included on his W-2 or his self-employment taxes.

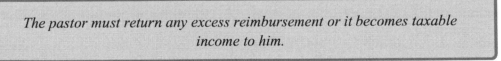

The pastor must return any excess reimbursement or it becomes taxable income to him.

Now that we've discussed the pieces, let's discuss how to structure the package. The total value of the compensation will be based on what your church can afford and what the IRS deems as a reasonable and appropriate compensation.

For example, let's assume your church can afford a $37,000 total compensation package for your minister. The church council and the pastor will need to consider several things as they work together to determine the best split between the three portions. I've designed a worksheet (on opposite page) to show some of the impacts.

	A	B	C	D	E	F
1			Your Church			
2			Minister Salary Worksheet			
3						
4	Cash Compensation				Federal Taxable Amount	Self-Employment Taxable Amount
5	Salary		15,000		15,000	15,000
6	Housing Allowance		15,000			15,000
7	Social Security Offset	7.65%	1,148		1,148	1,148
8	Total Cash Compensation			31,148	16,148	31,148
10	Benefits Compensation					
11	Health		3,600			
12	Retirement	5.0%	750			
13	Total Benefits Compensation			4,350	-	-
15	Reimbursements for Job-Related Costs (1)					
16	Mileage		400			
17	Conventions		500			
18	Continuing Education		500			
19	Books/Supplies		102			
20	Total Reimbursements			1,502	0	0
22	Total			$ 37,000	$ 16,148	$ 31,148
23						
24	Self-Employment tax	15.3%		$ 4,766		
25	Federal Income tax (2)	15.0%		$ 2,422		
26	Total Expected taxes			$ 7,188		
27						
28	(1) assumes a documented, accountable reimbursement plan.					
29	(2) Change based on your specific pastor's expected tax rate.					

In the first example, the minister has an equal split between **Salary** and **Housing Allowance**. The **Social Security Offset** is calculated on the salary portion only. Churches sometimes offer it as the pastor has to pay both the employee portion of Social Security and Medicare as well as the employer portion. A problem with this approach is income and self-employment taxes will be charged on the offset amount.

The benefits compensation components are assumed to be part of *tax-free plans*. Tax-free plans are IRS approved programs to allow the employee to receive the value of the benefit without paying taxes on it. In this example, the

Retirement plan has a formula to calculate 5% of the **Salary** figure. The church cannot use the housing allowance in calculating for retirement plans.

The job-related reimbursements should be calculated using the best estimates and assumptions available. If you want the pastor to represent your congregation at a convention, be sure to add the funds for it. Most importantly, make certain your church has a documented accountable reimbursement plan, or these items may become taxable income to him.

Perhaps after reviewing this with the pastor, he requests the **Housing Allowance** be increased to $25,000 as he has allowed housing expenses to support that amount. The spreadsheet can be adjusted to increase the housing allowance and decrease the salary to still stay with the $37,000 total package.

	A	B	C	D	E	F
1			Your Church			
2			Minister Salary Worksheet			
3						
4	Cash Compensation				Federal Taxable Amount	Self-Employment Taxable Amount
5	Salary		6,125		6,125	6,125
6	Housing Allowance		25,000			25,000
7	Social Security Offset	7.65%	469		469	469
8	Total Cash Compensation			31,594	6,594	31,594
10	Benefits Compensation					
11	Health		3,600			
12	Retirement	5.0%	306			
13	Total Benefits Compensation			3,906	-	-
15	Reimbursements for Job-Related Costs (1)					
16	Mileage		400			
17	Conventions		500			
18	Continuing Education		500			
19	Books/Supplies		100			
20	Total Reimbursements			1,500	0	0
22	Total			$ 37,000	$ 6,594	$ 31,594
23						
24	Self-Employment tax	15.3%		$ 4,834		
25	Federal Income tax (2)	15.0%		$ 989		
26	Total Expected taxes			$ 5,823		
27						
28	(1) assumes a documented, accountable reimbursement plan.					
29	(2) change based on your specific pastor's expected tax rate.					

As you can see on the spreadsheet, with this change, the pastor may like to see the **Total Expected Taxes** decreased by $1365, from $7188 to $5823, but his **Retirement** benefit has also decreased from $750 to $306.

If he can't fully substantiate the full $25,000 **Housing Allowance**, the excess must be treated as regular income on his taxes, but he would have missed out on the 5% of retirement for that excess.

Your church's situation may not need all of these components or may have other specific items to address in the compensation package. Add line items as needed and play around with the options.

Another item to keep in mind while computing the package is the traditions of love offerings in your church. As was discussed in Chapter XII, love offerings are often considered income for the minister. When the IRS is determining if the minister is receiving a reasonable pay for his services, they may take these love offerings into account. You will need to decide if love offering need to be included when computing the compensation package.

Growing churches sometimes want to compensate pastors based on a percentage of contributions. On freechurchaccounting.com, Vickey has the following advice for churches considering this:

> *I have heard very different opinions on this issue. Many years ago, I attended a church tax conference. The speaker stated that paying a pastor a percentage of the church's income would endanger the church's tax exempt status and may also cause the IRS to impose excise taxes on the clergy because it would fall under the private inurement and private benefit regulations.*

> *I cannot find anything to prove or disprove that statement. However, in the Church and Clergy Tax Guide, Richard Hammar, attorney, CPA, and author, states, "Churches are free to pay their clergy reasonable compensation for services rendered. Compensation packages based on a percentage of income are 'reasonable' and appropriate so long as the amount of compensation paid to a clergy under such an arrangement is in fact **reasonable in amount**."*

> *So if your church decides to or is already paying your pastor a percentage of the church's income, you should do 3 very important things:*

> - *Research the legality of paying the percentage. (Seek the advice of a qualified tax professional.)*

- *Make sure it is considered reasonable compensation for your pastor in regards to the size of your church's income and location.*

- *Put a cap on the amount, and that cap must be recorded in the minutes. Without a cap, any amount paid, no matter how small, would be considered private inurement and excessive benefit transactions, which could threaten your church's tax exempt status. The IRS could also impose penalties on your pastor and church leaders.*

  Whether you pay a percentage of income or more commonly a set amount, the total compensation MUST be considered "reasonable"!

The *private inurement regulations* Vickey refers to are the tax rules regarding transactions when a person in the church personally acquires economic gain through the use of funds or assets of the church. This can result in an *excess benefit*. An excess benefit is something which furthers the interest of an individual instead of the interest of the church.

The IRS can penalize the church by taking away its nonprofit status or charge significant fees for up to 200 percent times the excess benefit if it believes there has been a private inurement. The most common examples of situations that draw IRS penalties are the excess compensation package (too much economic benefit to the pastor for the services rendered) and transferring property to insiders for less than fair market value (giving a car to the minister, but not including it in his wages).

I.   Summary

Paying a minister is different than paying a regular employee. The church needs to determine who can be treated as a minister, how to determine if they are an employee or independent contractor, and understand the rules regarding the housing allowance.

Social Security and Medicare taxes are NOT deducted from a minister's paycheck. He needs to file and pay quarterly self-employment taxes.

Housing allowance is not considered part of the minister's earnings for federal income tax withholding purposes, but the minister must pay self-employment taxes on the allowance.

At year end, the minister's W-2 reflects his salary (not the housing allowance) and no earnings in the Social Security and Medicare boxes.

To develop the best compensation package for the minister and the church, research reasonable rates for his services, understand his housing costs, have a documented accountable reimbursement plan, cap any contingent earnings, and review everything with a tax specialist before finalizing.

XIII. Budgeting for Churches

So many people dread the concept of budgeting. I don't know if it's because I'm an accountant (and maybe a bit of a geek) or just odd, but I find budgeting the most interesting part of the accounting process. Think of preparing an annual budget as a way to require the church to consider the priorities of its congregation. There is a limit to the donations expected to be received, and therefore also a limit to the services that can be offered. The budgeting process can assist with the prioritization of your church's goals.

> *Approach the budgeting process as a way to get consensus around the priorities of your church.*

In this chapter, you will learn:

- The process necessary to prepare a budget
- How to do monthly budgeting
- The difference between budgets and forecasts
- How to use your forecast for analyzing cash flow

A. The Budget Process

Budgets are typically done on operating income and expenses. Income and expenses outside of normal church operations (non-operating income and expenses, like the receipt of a bequest or repaving the parking lot) only need to be budgeted if they are substantial. Budgets may be helpful for specific grants or funds (say a new building project) in which there will be numerous transaction and cash implications.

The budget process will have several steps. First you must consider if you need budgets at a top level (total church only) or program by program. Budgeting at the program level will take more time, but will also give you more information.

You may also wish to budget by program and grant. If you prepare program budgets for all areas (including administration), this will then be summarized into a total church budget.

Next, you will need to determine what donations and other revenues you are expecting. Unless your membership and contributions are stable, this is often difficult to budget. Economic factors, like the unemployment rate in your area or changes in the stock market, may impact your members' giving. If your church membership and donations have been fairly consistent over the years, use historical trends and tweak them for any likely changes and economic conditions.

For example, if pledges have consistently been close to $50,000 for the last five years, you are probably safe budgeting $50,000 for next year. But if a large donor moved to another state, consider reducing the expected pledges by their usual donation.

Some churches prefer to ask for the annual pledge or tithing commitments before they begin the budgeting process. This gives the treasurer a fairly accurate idea of the minimum amount of donations that will be received. The difficulty with this approach is the timing. If you start asking members for their commitments in October, it may be late December before you have them nailed down.

A hybrid approach is to use historical data and update it with known pledges before you finalize the budgets. This incorporates the best of both worlds and also allows the treasurer to do what accountants call a "smell test." A smell test really means "does it make sense?" If pledges committed are 50% less than last year's, but membership is stable, you either have an entry error or need to follow up with your members to see what has changed.

Non-pledged donations are usually budgeted at historical rates. This would include money received in the collection plate, memorials, rent, etc. Investment income can be budgeted based on expected returns of the investments. If you have $100,000 in a money market account that is currently paying 2% interest, you would budget $2000 of investment income.

For the expense budgets, I like to get buy-in from the heads of the programs. Start by giving a report to the directors of each program showing how much money they have spent this year.

Then, ask your program heads to submit their budget proposal of expected needs for the next year, and if it is substantially different than this year, an explanation should be included. I refer to this as the wish list. Be sure to remind the directors it is not part of the budget until approved by the finance committee or governing board.

Preparing their proposal and explanation encourages the program directors to think about what they would like to do differently. The written documentation is a good resource for the governing board as they deliberate on how to divide the budget dollars. This also gives you the information to put in your budget.

Besides program expenses, your church has facilities and other overhead expenditures. These can usually be calculated based on historical information or contracts. If you are allocating this expense across the programs, save yourself time by waiting until all of the direct program costs have been budgeted. Then you can do a one-time calculation based on percentage of space used, number of employees, or percentage of total costs to allocate the overhead.

For example, use a spreadsheet to estimate all of your building expenses. If you have three programs, Administration, Worship, and Education, you would add one third of the expected building expenses to each of these three budgets. You can do the same thing for salaries if you allocate people over more than one program. Some churches use different allocation percentages for facilities costs versus supplies and administrative costs.

Vickey's website has over 500 pages of questions and comments, but the question which generated the most comments was:

"What is the average % of salaries in a church budget?"

The consensus seems to be there is no consensus, but make sure that the compensation is reasonable for the services provided as excess compensation may jeopardize the tax exempt status of the church.

B.   Example Budget Spreadsheet

Vickey's free spreadsheet includes a top-level budget spreadsheet. There is a screenshot on the following page. Input your prior year amounts for each account in the 2013 column. The 2014 column is for your current budget. The next column assumes the budget should be spread evenly throughout the year, so there is a formula to divide the 2014 by 12 and multiply it by the number of months you are reporting on. This allows you to compare it to the actual income and expenses that have been recorded year to date as they are summarized in the final column.

			2013	2014	31-Jan-14	2014
9	**Revenue Accounts**					
10	1001	Plate Offering / Tithe /			$ -	$ -
11	1002	Covenant Missions			$ -	$ -
12	1003	Marco Missions Support			$ -	$ -
13	1004	Presbytery Support			$ -	$ -
14	1005	Not Assigned			$ -	$ -
15	1006	External Support / Fundraising & Unknown (faith)			$ -	$ -
16	1007	Support - Covenant Members			$ -	$ -
17	1008	Transfer - into Bank 1 from Bank 2			$ -	$ -
18	1009	Transfer - out of Bank 2 to Bank 1			$ -	$ -
19		**Total Revenue:**	$ -	$ -	$ -	$ -
21	**Expenses:**					
22	2001	Pastor Salary			$ -	$ -
23	2002	Pastor Housing			$ -	$ -
24	2003	Pastor's Ministry & Continuing Education Expenses			$ -	$ -
25	2004	Travel & Travel Allowance			$ -	$ -
26	2005	Music & Worship Program & Materials			$ -	$ -
27	2006	Christian Education Materials & Supplies			$ -	$ -
28	2007	Pulpit Supply			$ -	$ -
29	2008	Audio Visual and other Equipment			$ -	$ -
30	2009	Ministry Support			$ -	$ -
31	2011	Special Events and Projects			$ -	$ -
32	2012	Intern Program			$ -	$ -
33	2013	Missions & Presbytery			$ -	$ -
34	2014	Outside Services, Accounting, Legal, etc.			$ -	$ 40
35	2021	Office Supplies, stationary, postage, misc.			$ -	$ 30
36	2022	Computer costs and supplies			$ -	$ -
37	2023	Communications - Internet & Telephones			$ -	$ -
38	2024	Unassigned			$ -	$ -
39	2031	Janitorial Supplies and Services			$ -	$ -
40	2032	Repair and Maintenance - (Non-Covenant)			$ -	$ -
41	2033	Insurance - Liability			$ -	$ -
42	2034	Use Agreement (Utilities & Maint. Reserve)			$ -	$ -
44	2041	Food & Beverages			$ -	$ -
45	2042	Other Hospitality Related - Incl. Business Lunches, etc			$ -	$ -
46	2043	Unassigned			$ -	$ -
49	2061	Overdraft Charges			$ -	$ -
50		**Total Expenses:**	$ -	$ -	$ -	$ 70
52	**Net : Income Gain / (Loss)**		$ -	$ -	$ -	$ (70.00)
54	**Cash End of Period**					$ (70.00)

Historical data goes here.

Will be populated with actual data automatically.

C.   Monthly Budgeting

Your church's income may not be received equally throughout the year. Contributions are probably higher around Easter and Christmas and lower in the summer as people are traveling. Though salaries are usually stable through the year, there may be significant expenses in certain months. For example, if your church sends several people to a large conference in the summer or you have a vacation bible school, you may have additional expenses those months.

A strong monthly budget can help the church administrators plan for resources and cash flow. It also gives them a better understanding of how the church is doing compared to their budget at any point in the year.

> *A church was concerned that by the end of June they had only recieved 40% of their budgeted contributions. At that run rate, they risked running out of cash and having to lay off staff. But by going back three years and tracking contributions by month, they noticed that 10% were typically received in the same month as Easter and 32% of the contributions were received in December. Using this information, they realized they were likely on track to reach their budget goals and did not need to reduce their staff.*

If you have historical data, use it to track your contributions. For your members who tithe, budget their gifts based on how they would like to pay—weekly, monthly, quarterly, or annually. Plate income and other non-pledged support are harder to nail down, but historical trends should help.

For expenses, consider in which month they are most likely to occur. As you are probably using the cash basis method of accounting, you will need to budget the expense when you think the bill will be paid. If vacation bible school supplies are typically ordered and paid two months before the summer, budget the expense in April, not June. If each September, the church requires the professional landscaper to prepare the lawn for winter, but the bill doesn't usually come until October, budget the expense for October.

Most computerized software packages, like QuickBooks, allow you to design budgets down to the program level by month. This allows you to run reports monthly, quarterly, or annually at the top level or by individual program.

A well-thought-out monthly budget is more work, but it can also be a strong internal control and give the pastor and governing council a feel for changes in the congregation. Revenue coming in below expectations may be due to unhappy members or fraud. The church would not know to investigate without this information. Large unbudgeted expenses could be related to growth at the church, a program director who is not following protocol, or even theft. The administrators of the church need to understand which.

> *If reviewed regularly with the pastor and governing council, monthly budgets are instrumental in understanding the financial situation of the church.*

D. Forecasts

No matter how carefully and thoughtfully you work through your budget, situations may change. To help you anticipate what these changes will mean for your church, you may want to prepare a forecast.

Budgets are typically created annually and stay stable throughout the year. *Forecasts* are used as a "what if" tool and are useful when change is anticipated. A forecast is not meant to replace the budget, but to give the administration tools to understand and plan for changes before they occur.

Perhaps you are considering hiring some new personnel to run an expanded children's program. You could create a forecast making assumptions on the additional costs of payroll and program expenses offset by any anticipated growth in your organization.

To create a forecast, I like to start with a schedule of current actual income and expenses year to date. Input these in a summary fashion in a spreadsheet. Add columns for the remaining months of the year and populate those columns with the budgeted data.

Next, change the budgeted amounts for the items you know will be changing. For example, if you expect a gift which will fund half of a new youth leader, increase the budget for contributions by the amount of the gift in the month you expect the money and increase salaries, benefits, and payroll taxes for the cost of the new position.

Anytime you are forecasting for new staff, do not forget to add any additional expenses, i.e. a cell phone, computer, desk, additional supplies the person may need. It is a common error to only think of the monthly salary, not the associated day-to-day costs of doing his job.

Once you have adjusted for known items, take a look at your run rate. The *run rate* is the average actual cost of each account. If the run rate for telephone is $300, and you have only budgeted $200 per month for the rest of the year, consider whether you need to increase the budgeted amount for your forecast. Run rate analysis can be very useful but requires careful evaluation.

If you are already using Vickey's spreadsheet, the data for the year has populated each month. If not, you can type in your own information of revenue received and expenses paid. In the remaining months, key in your budget. In the example below, I added three columns, Budget, Expected Variance, and Actual Run Rate.

	January Actual	February Actual	[Septe]mber Forecast	October Forecast	November Forecast	December Forecast	Total YTD	Budget	Expected Variance	Actual Run Rate
Cash Beginning of P	4,000	2,333	3,367	1,275	(317)	(1,408)	4,000			
Revenue										
# Plate Offering / Tit	1,000	2,000	2,000	2,500	3,000	5,000	35,000	30,000	5,000	2,000
# Covenant Missions										
# Marco Missions Support							-		-	-
# Presbytery Support							-		-	-
Total Revenue:	1,000	2,000	2,000	2,500	3,000	5,000	35,000	30,000	5,000	2,000
Expenses:										
# Pastor Salary	1,667	1,667	1,667	1,667	1,667	1,667	20,000	20,000	-	1,667
# Pastor Housing							-		-	-
# Pastor's Ministry							-		-	-
# Travel & Travel							-		-	-
# Music & Worship F	1,000	800	875	875	875	875	10,500	10,000	500	875
# Christian Education			300	300	300	300	1,500		1,500	-
# Pulpit Supply							-		-	-
# Equipment							-		-	-
# Ministry Support							-		-	-
# Special Events							-		-	-
# Office Supplies							-		-	-
# Computer supplies							-		-	-
# Communications							-		-	-
# Youth Leader			1,250	1,250	1,250	1,250	7,500		7,500	-
# Janitorial Supplies							-		-	-
# Repair and Maintenance							-		-	-
# Van Insurance							-		-	-
# Overdraft Charges							-		-	-
Total Expenses:	2,667	2,467	4,092	4,092	4,092	4,092	39,500	3?,000	9,500	2,542
Net Balance: Gain /	(1,667)	(467)	(2,09?)	(1,592)	(1,092)	908	(4,500)		(4,500)	(542)
Cash End of Period	2,333	1,867	1,275	(317)	(1,408)	(500)	(500)	-	(4,500)	(542)

The Actual Run Rate column sums up all of the months with revenue and expenses that have occurred and divides it by that number of months to give an average revenue or expense for the periods. Use this calculation to see if your monthly budget numbers look reasonable. For example, if the run rate for Music and Worship is $875 per month and the budget is $700 per month, you may need to investigate if there were unusual expenses in the first months or if the budget was simply too low.

To develop a forecast:

- Adjust the budget column numbers to the most likely amounts you will be spending based on your current run rate and experience.

- Adjusted any numbers you expect to change based on changing conditions or expected donations or expense.

- Look at the column titled **Expected Variance**. Are you substantially over or under in any category?

- If you are substantially worse than budget, use the forecast as a tool to determine the best way to get closer to your budgeted goals.

The earlier you can make the church administration aware of potential financial shortfalls, the earlier they can address the issues.

E.   Cash Flow Analysis

The forecast can also be used to help track cash flow. If you are a small church, you probably use the cash basis of accounting (i.e. only record revenue and expenses when the cash is received or paid out). With a well-thought-out forecast, the cash requirements can be tracked. With advance warning that the cash flow will not be sufficient, the church can apply for a line of credit, have additional fundraisers, or put off non-critical purchases.

The worksheet from the previous example also takes the beginning cash balance and adjusts it for the expected expenses. It appears the church will run out of money in October and have a $500 cash shortfall for the year.

Using this information can help you determine the best approach to guard against cash shortfalls and plan for contingencies.

F.   Summary

You should now understand how to go through the budget process and break it out into monthly increments. Throughout the year, you will be able to update this information into a forecast and a cash-flow analysis that will guide your church's growing and evolving ministries.

The transactions have been entered and budgets and forecasts prepared. Let's look at month-end financial requirements.

XIV. Month-End Financial Requirements

It's the end of the month and your monthly church council meeting is coming up. There are things you will want to do to assure the financial information you give them is accurate and complete. In this chapter, we will:

- Review the steps needed to assure complete financials
- Learn how to reconcile the bank accounts
- Learn what reports to generate for comprehensive information

A.   Monthly Processes for Complete Financials

Before we can put together any financial reports for the pastor, treasurer, or governing council, we need to assure the information is complete and accurate. At a minimum, you will need to:

- Check unopened mail for any checks or donations received and for any unpaid bills.
- Make sure all contributions have been deposited in the bank and recorded in the financial records.
- All paid bills should be recorded in the appropriate expense account and against the checking account.
- Payroll should be recorded and payroll liabilities paid to the appropriate agencies.
- Record credit card charges to the correct expense accounts.
- Look at your bank statement and record interest earned, bank charges, and any automatic withdrawals into the correct accounts.
- If you allow online donations, record the donations received less the processing charge.

B.   Bank Reconciliation

Once all transactions have been recorded, you will need to reconcile your bank account. This is the process of determining what you have in your records that the bank has not yet recorded or what has cleared the bank but has not yet been recorded by you. It is a simple process, but can be very tedious.

Start with the bank statement.

- Scan the *Other Withdrawals, Debits,* and *Service Charges* section of the statement and make sure each of the charges have been properly recorded in your general ledger account. If you don't know what a charge is for, call the bank immediately. Banks rarely make mistakes, but they do make them. If you do not bring it to the bank's attention on a timely basis, you may lose any recourse.

- Look at the deposits that have cleared the bank and compare them to the deposits recorded in the general ledger cash account. Sometimes the last deposits of the month are not yet recorded in the bank. These are called *outstanding deposits*. If it appears to be a timing issue, it should not be a problem.

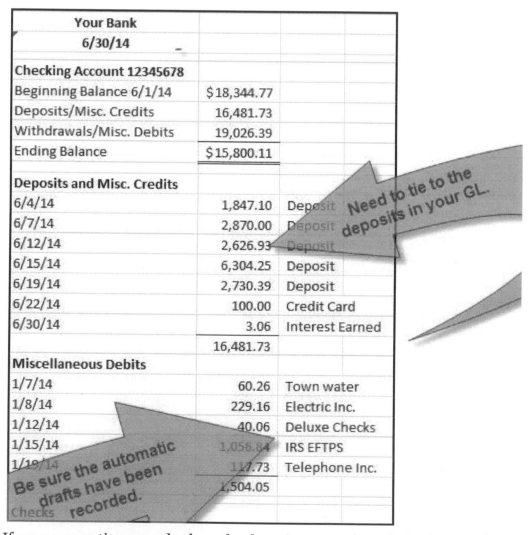

Your Bank 6/30/14			
Checking Account 12345678			
Beginning Balance 6/1/14	$18,344.77		
Deposits/Misc. Credits	16,481.73		
Withdrawals/Misc. Debits	19,026.39		
Ending Balance	$15,800.11		
Deposits and Misc. Credits			
6/4/14	1,847.10	Deposit	Need to tie to the deposits in your GL.
6/7/14	2,870.00	Deposit	
6/12/14	2,626.93	Deposit	
6/15/14	6,304.25	Deposit	
6/19/14	2,730.39	Deposit	
6/22/14	100.00	Credit Card	
6/30/14	3.06	Interest Earned	
	16,481.73		
Miscellaneous Debits			
1/7/14	60.26	Town water	
1/8/14	229.16	Electric Inc.	
1/12/14	40.06	Deluxe Checks	
1/15/14	1,056.84	IRS EFTPS	Be sure the automatic drafts have been recorded.
1/19/14	117.73	Telephone Inc.	
	1,504.05		
Checks			

If your accounting records show the deposit was made early in the month, you need to research why the bank is not showing it. It could be a bank error, it could be recorded in the accounting system incorrectly, or the deposit may never have been made. It may even be sitting in a church counter's car where he forgot about it.

Less frequently, there will be deposits recorded by the bank but not in the accounting records. The most common of these is credit card donations. If your website allows donors to make donations online, the credit card processor may automatically move the money into your checking account. In this case, go to the website donation site and print out a report by donor and amount for the month. Record these donations and restart your bank reconciliation.

- Compare each of the checks you wrote to the checks that cleared the bank. List any checks not on the bank statement as an *outstanding check*. If there are checks on the bank statement that are not in the accounting records, you will need to investigate these. Were they properly approved and signed by an authorized signer? If so, why weren't they recorded?

Once you know the outstanding deposits and checks, you are ready to complete the reconciliation.

	A	B	C	D	E
2		**Bank Reconciliation**			
3					
4	Date				
5	06/30/2014	Bank Balance from Statement		$	5,789.14
6		Outstanding Deposits			
7	06/29/2014			150.00	
8	06/30/2014			1,250.00	
9					
10	Total Outstanding Deposits				1,400.00
11					
12		Outstanding Checks	Check Number		
13	06/15/2014	Jane Smith	1052	25.00	
14	06/20/2014	USPS	1061	37.00	
15	06/28/2014	Utility Inc.	1075	125.00	
16	06/29/2014	Pastor Jim (payroll)	1076	1,250.00	
17					
18	Total Outstanding Checks				(1,437.00)
19		Ending Book Balance *		$	5,752.14
20					
21	*This should be your general ledger cash account balance.				
22	If it doesn't tie, make sure all of the bank charges and withdrawals have been recorded.				

- Set up a spreadsheet and input the ending balance from the bank statement.

- Add to this balance the outstanding deposits.

- Subtract any outstanding checks. The net effect should be the balance of the cash account in your accounting records.

If it does NOT equal the accounting records, you will need to go back through everything that was recorded in the general ledger and everything that was recorded in the bank. A common error is in transposition (the check was written for $93.00 but recorded in the accounting records as $39.00). If the amount you are off is divisible by 9, it is likely to be a transposition. You will need to compare each check and deposit to the bank statement to find it.

If outstanding checks from the previous month still have not cleared, your reconciliation will not balance. Look at the previous reconciliation and verify that all checks on the outstanding list have cleared this month. If not, add the un-cleared check to the outstanding checks list.

Great! Now you have the bank and accounting record reconciled. But you aren't quite done.

- Look at the reconciling items for outdated or unusual items. In the example above, we aren't surprised to see Pastor Jim's payroll check outstanding because we gave it to him on the last day of the month and he didn't have time to get to the bank. But Jane Smith was reimbursed for some expenses and said she needed the money right away. You may want to call her to see if the check was lost or if it is still in her purse.

- Be sure to reconcile the petty cash fund and any gift cards. Petty cash is reconciled by totaling the receipts and counting the remaining cash as discussed in Chapter VIII. Gift card holders should have receipts for any reduction in the value of the gift card. Record the receipts in the appropriate expense categories.

The completed bank reconciliation with the bank statement and cleared checks (or bank images) should be given to the pastor or treasurer each month for review. They should scrutinize the checks for unusual payees and beware of long-outstanding checks or deposits.

C.   Investment Account Reconciliations

If your church holds funds in an investment account with a broker, you should receive statements monthly or quarterly. These need to be reconciled in a similar manner to the checking account. The most significant difference is the income earned on the account.

Most investment accounts will list several types of income: interest, dividend, realized gain or loss from sale of stock, and unrealized gain or loss based on market value. The *interest* and *dividends* are recorded in the general ledger in operating income accounts called Interest and Dividends.

Realized gain or loss from the sale of stock is the money change in value of the investment based on the sale of some of the stock. The gain or loss is treated as Other Income/Loss and is usually shown at the bottom of the Income Statement. It is differentiated from the regular income as it is not from donations or services offered to donors.

Unrealized gain or loss reflects the change in market value of the stock since the last brokerage statements. It should be recorded in a separate Other Income or Loss accounts (usually called **Unrealized Gain/Loss**. This income is considered unrealized as the stock has not been sold, so its value will change with the stock market.

D.   Generate Reports

Once the bank statement is reconciled, it is time to start looking at the financial reports. I like to start with a balance sheet. The *balance sheet* is a snapshot of the church's current financial situation. It list the assets (the things owned), the liabilities (those owed), and the net assets (the cumulative amount of what's left). The balance sheet can be as simple as the example on the next page. Or, if the church is using the accrual basis of accounting, it may look more like the balance sheet from the sample nonprofit organization in QuickBooks shown in the second example.

Either way, review each line item on the balance sheet. Any cash and investment accounts should have reconciliations. An aging of the amounts owed to the church as receivable should be compared to the amount on the balance sheet. The fixed assets (equipment, land, and buildings) should have a list of items to support the amount. The treasurer and/or pastor should have a detailed understanding of the items in any Other Assets category.

Your Church	
Basic Balance Sheet	
06/30/2014	
Assets	
Cash	$5,752.14
Petty Cash	100.00
Gift Cards	100.00
Computers	1,200.00
Total Assets	**$7,152.14**
Liabilities and Net Assets	
Payroll Taxes Due	$ 356.00
Unrestricted Net Assets	5,796.14
Temporarily Restricted Net Assets	1,000.00
Total Liabilities and Net Assets	**$7,152.14**

The liabilities should be identifiable and paid in a timely fashion. The *Net Assets* are divided between unrestricted (normal operating balances) and restricted (grants or designated programs).

We Care Community Foundation
Balance Sheet
As of December 15, 2018

	◇ Dec 15, 18 ◇
▼ ASSETS	
▼ Current Assets	
▶ Checking/Savings	401,095.38
▶ Accounts Receivable	496,590.00
▶ Other Current Assets	45,525.00
Total Current Assets	943,210.38
▶ Fixed Assets	99,050.00
▶ Other Assets	3,000.00
TOTAL ASSETS	1,045,260.38
▼ LIABILITIES & EQUITY	
▼ Liabilities	
▼ Current Liabilities	
▶ Accounts Payable	13,135.00
▶ Credit Cards	184.60
▶ Other Current Liabilities	▶ 74,586.34 ◀
Total Current Liabilities	87,905.94
Total Liabilities	87,905.94
▼ Equity	
▶ 3000 · Unrestricted net assets	(604,595.11)
3010 · Unrestrict (retained earnings)	228,136.52
▶ 3100 · Temporarily restrict net asset	574,595.11
▶ 3200 · Permanently restrict net assets	30,000.00
Net Income	729,217.92
Total Equity	957,354.44
TOTAL LIABILITIES & EQUITY	1,045,260.38

Once you feel the balance sheet is correct, it is time to review the *profit & loss* statement. The profit & loss statement reflects all the operating revenues and related expenses to give you the change in net assets. This can be looked at from a top-level basis as well as a program-by-program basis. Here is an example profit & loss by program from a QuickBooks file.

Your Church
Profit & Loss by Class
January through October 2013
Cash Basis

	100 Admini...	200 Worship	300 Educat...	300 Educat...	Total 300 E...	600 Fundra...	910 Unrestr...	920 Tempo...	Unclassified	TOTAL
Ordinary Income/Expense										
Income										
4100 · Pledges/Offerings	0.00	0.00	0.00	0.00	0.00	0.00	20,572.35	0.00	0.00	20,572.35
4200 · Fundraising Income	0.00	0.00	0.00	0.00	0.00	0.00	5,000.00	0.00	0.00	5,000.00
4300 · Other Operating Inco...	0.00	0.00	0.00	0.00	0.00	0.00	15.00	0.00	0.00	15.00
4400 · Income -Other Opera...	0.00	0.00	0.00	0.00	0.00	0.00	50.00	0.00		
5000 · Other Income-Non-O...	0.00	0.00	0.00	0.00	0.00	0.00	10.00	52,000.00		
Total Income	0.00	0.00	0.00	0.00	0.00	0.00	25,647.35	52,000.00		
Gross Profit	0.00	0.00	0.00	0.00	0.00	0.00	25,647.35	52,000.00		77,647.35
Expense										
6000 · Facilities-Utilities	250.00	0.00	0.00	0.00	0.00	0.00	0.00			250.00
6100 · Facilities-Other	0.00	0.00	0.00	0.00	0.00	0.00	0.00			0.00
6300 · Administrative Expen...	99.95	4.00	0.00	0.00	0.00	0.00	0.00			111.95
6400 · Payroll Expenses	5,000.00	8,000.00	0.00	0.00	0.00	0.00	0.00			
6500 · Employee Benefits	1,172.00	400.00	0.00	0.00	0.00	0.00	0.00			1,572.00
6600 · Program Expenses	0.00	175.35	25.00	0.00	25.00	0.00	0.00			200.35
7400 · Capital Campaign Ex...	0.00	0.00	0.00	0.00	0.00	250.00	0.00			250.00
Total Expense	6,521.95	8,579.35	25.00	0.00	33.00	250.00	0.00			
Net Ordinary Income	-6,521.95	-8,579.35	-25.00	0.00	-33.00	-250.00	25,647.35	52,000.00		263.05
Net Income	-6,521.95	-8,579.35	-25.00	0.00	-33.00	-250.00	25,647.35	52,000.00		52,263.05

Total ties to balance sheet.

The total net income will add to (or net loss will subtract from) the Net Assets area of the balance sheet.

The most useful review is the *Profit & Loss Comparison to Budget*. Depending on your accounting system, this can be as easy as the free option in Vickey's worksheet or a program-by-program comparison to budget which can be generated by computerized software systems.

Either way, it is important to understand any variances to the budget. If contributions are below expectations, you can research the issues and make appropriate adjustments. As we discussed in the previous chapter, the use of the comparison to budget report can be a powerful control.

A	B	C	D	E	F	G
		Note: Columns D & E are not protected and data can be entered. once data is entered it may be desirable to protect the columns.			Linear Budget YTD	YTD Actuals
			Actual	Budget	31-Jan-14	2014
			2013	2014		
	Revenue Accounts					
	1001	Plate Offering / Tithe /			$ -	$ -
	1002	Covenant Missions			$ -	$ -
	1003	Marco Missions Support			$ -	$ -
	1004	Presbytery Support			$ -	$ -
	1005	Not Assigned			$ -	$ -
	1006	External Support / Fundraising & Unknown (faith)			$ -	$ -
	1007	Support - Covenant Members			$ -	$ -
	1008	Transfer - into Bank 1 from Bank 2			$ -	$ -
	1009	Transfer - out of Bank 2 to Bank 1			$ -	$ -
		Total Revenue:	$ -	$ -	$ -	$ -
	Expenses:					
	2001	Pastor Salary			$ -	$ -
	2002	Pastor Housing			$ -	$ -
	2003	Pastor's Ministry & Continuing Education Expenses			$ -	$ -
	2004	Travel & Travel Allowance			$ -	$ -
	2005	Music & Worship Program & Materials			$ -	$ -
	2006	Christian Education Materials & Supplies			$ -	$ -
	2007	Pulpit Supply			$ -	$ -
	2008	Audio Visual and other Equipment			$ -	$ -
	2009	Ministry Support			$ -	$ -
	2011	Special Events and Projects			$ -	$ -
	2012	Intern Program			$ -	$ -
	2013	Missions & Presbytery			$ -	$ -
	2014	Outside Services, Accounting, Legal, etc.			$ -	$ -
	2021	Office Supplies, stationary, postage, misc.			$ -	$ -
	2022	Computer costs and supplies			$ -	$ -
	2023	Communications - Internet & Telephones			$ -	$ -
	2024	Unassigned			$ -	$ -
	2061	Overdraft Charges			$ -	$ -
		Total Expenses:	$ -	$ -	$ -	$ -
	Net : Income Gain / (Loss)		$ -	$ -	$ -	$ -

This would also be a good time to look at the forecast you prepared in the last chapter to give the governing board an understanding of the remainder of the rest of the year. If you track tithing and pledges as receivables, an *accounts receivable report* will show the treasurer which members still have outstanding balances.

We Care Community Foundation
A/R Aging Summary
As of December 15, 2018

	Current	1 - 30	31 - 60	61 - 90	> 90	TOTAL
Bayshore City Schools	855.00	0.00	0.00	0.00	0.00	855.00
Easley, Paula						
Mexico Trip	250.00	0.00	0.00	0.00	0.00	250.00
Total Easley, Paula	250.00	0.00	0.00	0.00	0.00	250.00
HHS						
Research Next Year	250,000.00	0.00	0.00	0.00	0.00	250,000.00
StudentEd Next Year	200,000.00	0.00	0.00	0.00	0.00	200,000.00
Total HHS	450,000.00	0.00	0.00	0.00	0.00	450,000.00
Lamb, Brad	15,035.00	0.00	0.00	0.00	0.00	15,035.00
Lucchini, Bill	15,000.00	0.00	0.00	0.00	0.00	15,000.00
Oliveri, Tom						
Job 1	200.00	0.00	0.00	0.00	0.00	200.00
Mexico Trip	250.00	0.00	0.00	0.00	0.00	250.00
Total Oliveri, Tom	450.00	0.00	0.00	0.00	0.00	450.00
Phillip Foundation						
Phillip This Year	60,000.00	0.00	0.00	0.00	0.00	60,000.00
Phillip Foundation - Other	0.00	0.00	0.00	0.00	(60,000.00)	(60,000.00)
Total Phillip Foundation	60,000.00	0.00	0.00	0.00	(60,000.00)	0.00
Tumacder, Jacint	15,000.00	0.00	0.00	0.00	0.00	15,000.00
TOTAL	556,590.00	0.00	0.00	0.00	(60,000.00)	496,590.00

This assortment of reports should give your pastor and treasurer a complete understanding of the financial situation of the church.

> *Talk to your pastor, treasurer, and governing council to determine the information they would like to see. The reports can then be designed around their requirements.*

E. Summary

Closing out the month can be nerve-racking, but you now have the tools to know what to look for and how to make sure everything has been recorded. In the appendix, I've included the Month-End Checklist I designed for QuickBooks users. Feel free to use it as a guide and adjust for your particular situation.

We have also reviewed how to prepare bank reconciliations, reconcile brokerage accounts, and generate the monthly reports. Next, we'll be reviewing how to handle year-end requirements.

XV. Year-end and Audit Issues

At the end of the calendar year, there are a few more things to do. In this chapter we will cover how to:

- Complete and file year-end payroll forms to employees and the government.
- Complete and file forms for independent contractors.
- Send year-end donor acknowledgements.
- Review possible state-required filings.
- Assess potential audit needs.

A.   Forms W-2 and W-3

In the chapter on payroll, we discussed the W-2s that must be sent to employees and the W-3 to send a copy of the W-2s to the Social Security Administration. For non-employees, you will need to send 1099s. Details on completing the forms are in Chapter XI.

B.   Form 944, Employer's ANNUAL Federal Tax Return

This is an annual return for employers with very little payroll and is used in lieu of the quarterly 941s. It can ONLY be used if the IRS has notified you in writing. See Chapter XI for the requirements.

It is a two-page form and is similar to the 941. Input the wages paid for the year and the related taxes. If the total taxes are greater than $2500, you will need to show the monthly amounts.

Be sure to sign, title, and date before mailing. If you have not deposited the taxes, use the voucher at the end of the form.

Form **944** for 2013: **Employer's ANNUAL Federal Tax Return**

Department of the Treasury — Internal Revenue Service

OMB No. 1545-2007

Employer identification number (EIN)

Name (not your trade name)

Trade name (if any)

Address

Number   Street   Suite or room number

City   State   ZIP code

Foreign country name   Foreign province/county   Foreign postal code

Who Must File Form 944

You must file annual Form 944 instead of filing quarterly Forms 941 only if the IRS notified you in writing.

Instructions and prior-year forms are available at www.irs.gov/form944.

Read the separate instructions before you complete Form 944. Type or print within the boxes.

Part 1: Answer these questions for this year. Employers in American Samoa, Guam, the Commonwealth of the Northern Mariana Islands, the U.S. Virgin Islands, and Puerto Rico can skip lines 1 and 2.

1   Wages, tips, and other compensation   1

2   Federal income tax withheld from wages, tips, and other compensation   2

3   If no wages, tips, and other compensation are subject to social security or Medicare tax   ☐ Check and go to line 5.

4   Taxable social security and Medicare wages and tips:

Column 1

4a   Taxable social security wages   × .124 =

4b   Taxable social security tips   × .124 =

4c   Taxable Medicare wages & tips   × .029 =

4d   Taxable wages & tips subject to Additional Medicare Tax withholding   × .009 =

Do NOT include the minister's wages here.

4e   Add Column 2 from lines 4a, 4b, 4c, and 4d 4e

5   Total taxes before adjustments. Add lines 2 and 4e   5

6   Current year's adjustments (see instructions)   6

7   Total taxes after adjustments. Combine lines 5 and 6   7

8   Total deposits for this year, including overpayment applied from a prior year and overpayments applied from Form 944-X, 944-X (PR), 944-X (SP), 941-X, or 941-X (PR) . .   8

9a   COBRA premium assistance payments (see instructions) 9a

9b   Number of individuals provided COBRA premium assistance

10   Add lines 8 and 9a   10

11   Balance due. If line 7 is more than line 10, enter the difference and see instructions   11

12   Overpayment. If line 10 is more than line 7, enter the difference   Check one: ☐ Apply to next return. ☐ Send a refund.

▶ You MUST complete both pages of Form 944 and SIGN it.   Next ➡

For Privacy Act and Paperwork Reduction Act Notice, see the back of the Payment Voucher.   Cat. No. 39316N   Form **944** (2013)

Name *(not your trade name)*	Employer identification number (EIN)

Part 2: Tell us about your deposit schedule and tax liability for this year.

13 Check one: ☐ Line 7 is less than $2,500. Go to Part 3.

☐ Line 7 is $2,500 or more. Enter your tax liability for each month. If you are a semiweekly depositor or you accumulate $100,000 or more of liability on any day during a deposit period, you must complete Form 945-A instead of the boxes below.

	Jan.			Apr.			Jul.			Oct.	
13a		.	13d		.	13g		.	13j		.
	Feb.			May			Aug.			Nov.	
13b		.	13e		.	13h		.	13k		.
	Mar.			Jun.			Sep.			Dec.	
13c		.	13f		.	13i		.	13l		.

Total liability for year. Add lines 13a through 13l. Total must equal line 7.　13m

Part 3: Tell us about your business. If question 14 does NOT apply to your business, leave it blank.

14　If your business has closed or you stopped paying wages...

☐ Check here and enter the final date you paid wages.

Part 4: May we speak with your third-party designee?

Do you want to allow an employee, a paid tax preparer, or another person to discuss this return with the IRS? See the instructions for details.

☐ Yes. Designee's name and phone number

Select a 5-digit Personal Identification Number (PIN) to use when talking to IRS. ☐ ☐ ☐ ☐ ☐

☐ No.

Part 5: Sign Here. You MUST complete both pages of Form 944 and SIGN it.

Under penalties of perjury, I declare that I have examined this return, including accompanying schedules and statements, and to the best of my knowledge and belief, it is true, correct, and complete. Declaration of preparer (other than taxpayer) is based on all information of which preparer has any knowledge.

X **Sign your name here**

Print your name here

Print your title here

Date

Best daytime phone

Paid Preparer Use Only　　Check if you are self-employed ☐

Preparer's name		PTIN	
Preparer's signature		Date	
Firm's name (or yours if self-employed)		EIN	
Address		Phone	
City	State	ZIP code	

Page 2　　　　Form **944** (2013)

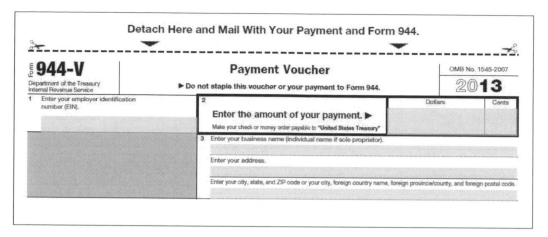

Detach Here and Mail With Your Payment and Form 944.

Form **944-V**	Payment Voucher	OMB No. 1545-2007
Department of the Treasury Internal Revenue Service	▶ Do not staple this voucher or your payment to Form 944.	2013

1 Enter your employer identification number (EIN).

2 Enter the amount of your payment. ▶

Make your check or money order payable to "**United States Treasury**"

| Dollars | Cents |

3 Enter your business name (individual name if sole proprietor).

Enter your address.

Enter your city, state, and ZIP code or your city, foreign country name, foreign province/county, and foreign postal code.

C. Form 1099

In Chapter X, we discussed the difference between employees and independent contractors. Non-employees may include a traveling pastor, your bookkeeper, plumber, or yard service. The IRS requires the church (and any other organization) to send independent contractors a Form 1099 after the end of the calendar year.

9595 ☐ VOID ☐ CORRECTED

PAYER'S name, street address, city or town, state or province, country, ZIP or foreign postal code, and telephone no.	1 Rents	OMB No. 1545-0115
	2 Royalties	2014
		Form 1099-MISC
	3 Other income $	4 Federal income tax withheld $
PAYER'S federal identification number	RECIPIENT'S identification number	5 Fishing boat proceeds $	6 Medical and health care payments $
RECIPIENT'S name	7 Nonemployee compensation $	8 Substitute payments in lieu of dividends or interest $
Street address (including apt. no.)	9 Payer made direct sales of $5,000 or more of consumer products to a buyer (recipient) for resale ▶ ☐	10 Crop insurance proceeds $
City or town, state or province, country, and ZIP or foreign postal code	11	12
Account number (see instructions)	2nd TIN not. ☐	13 Excess golden parachute payments $	14 Gross proceeds paid to an attorney $
15a Section 409A deferrals $	15b Section 409A income $	16 State tax withheld $	17 State/Payer's state no.	18 State income $

Miscellaneous Income

Copy A
For
Internal Revenue
Service Center

File with Form 1096.

For Privacy Act and Paperwork Reduction Act Notice, see the 2014 General Instructions for Certain Information Returns.

Form **1099-MISC**   Cat. No. 14425J   www.irs.gov/form1099misc   Department of the Treasury - Internal Revenue Service

Do Not Cut or Separate Forms on This Page — Do Not Cut or Separate Forms on This Page

If the person works for a corporation, i.e. the business name ends in "Inc.", you are not required to send a 1099. A possible exception to this is that all attorneys paid over $600 annually must receive a 1099.

Any person (not a corporation) whom the church paid over $600 (amount changes—check the IRS website), cumulatively, will need a 1099. Keep in mind this is cumulative, so be sure to total ALL payments through the year to them.

The PAYER on this form is the church and the RECIPIENT is the person who received the payments. The church's EIN goes in the PAYER's federal identification number box. Using the EIN or SSN from the W-9 (received from the contractor before you paid him—see Chapter X), fill in the RECIPIENT's identification number, name, and address.

Like the W-2, there is a red copy A to send to the government and several black copies. Copy B is for the recipient to use to fill out his tax return, and Copy C is for the church to retain and file. Copies 1 and 2 are for the state and local tax department and to be filed with the recipient's state and local tax returns, respectively, if required. The 1099s must be mailed to the recipients by January 31st of the following year.

D.   Form 1096

After mailing the black copies of the 1099 to the recipients, the red copy As are sent to the Internal Revenue Service along with a transmittal form 1096. The transmittal form summarizes the total number of 1099s and the total dollars reported.

This form is used to transmit other types of forms, so select the box labeled 1099-Misc 95 near the bottom. Fill in the church's name and address, the contact person (may be the bookkeeper), the telephone number, and the email. Only the church's Employer Identification Number needs to be listed unless the church does not have an EIN. Then the pastor or primary person's SSN is used. Box 3 asks for the total number of forms. Box 4 is usually 0, as the church probably did not withhold taxes on any payments. To compute the amount for box 5, add all of the amounts listed in Box 7 on the individual 1099s.

The form must be signed by an appropriate representative of the church with their title and date. The title bookkeeper is not considered an appropriate representative. Treasurer, pastor, and the head of the governing council are all considered representatives of the church.

Return this entire page to the Internal Revenue Service. Photocopies are not acceptable.

The form includes the address where the IRS requires the transmittal and the Copy As of the 1099s are to be sent. Make a complete copy for your records and file in a locked, secure location as these documents have sensitive information like SSNs.

All payroll and employee information, as well as W-9s, should be kept in a locked, secure location. It is not uncommon for employees, cleaning crews, or other workers to access the information for use in identity theft.

E.   Year-end Donor Acknowledgements

In Chapter V, we discussed the value and requirements of the donor acknowledgement. The church is not penalized for not acknowledging received gifts, except in the case of vehicles, but as the donor needs the acknowledgement for tax purposes, it should be considered a required mailing. Most charitable organizations send the acknowledgements out by January 31.

To refresh your memory, the donor acknowledgement must include:

- Name of the organization,
- Amount of cash contribution,
- Description (but not value) of non-cash contribution,
- Statement that goods or services, if any, that the organization provided in return for the contribution consisted entirely of intangible religious benefits, if that was the case, and
- Description and good faith estimate of the value of goods or services, if any, that the organization provided in return for the contribution.

> *As these acknowledgements are going to your donors, it would behoove you to include thanks and an explanation of the good their gifts have done.*

F.   State Filings

Each state has its own rules and filing requirements. You will need to research the payroll, income tax, sales tax, and license requirements in your particular state. If you are a registered 501(c)3, your state may require an annual filing. Check with the office of your Secretary of State. On my website, www.accountantbesideyou.com, I have a page with links to each state's website for your convenience.

G.   Audit Needs

EVERY church should have an audit each year. Having a CPA firm perform the audit is preferred, but may be cost prohibitive. Many churches use an audit committee instead. The audit committee should consist of people with some accounting knowledge not involved in the day-to-day accounting of the church. If your church is associated with a larger organization, there are probably audit committee guidelines. If not, check www.accountantbesideyou.com for a downloadable audit guide.

In preparation for the audit, the bookkeeper, treasurer, and/or pastor should do the following:

- For each **cash account**, look at the bank reconciliation and tie it to the balance on the Balance Sheet. While you have them out, take the time to look for checks that haven't cleared in months. Do you need to make some calls and reissue the checks? And don't forget to reconcile your petty cash and/or gift cards.

- **Investment account** statements should be compared to the balance sheet. If the ending balance does not match, you probably need to record interest earned and any investment income or loss.

- Print an *aging schedule* for each of your **receivable accounts**. An aging schedule is a list of money due to the church by age. Any old receivables should be reviewed to see if follow up is needed or if they should be written off. Also think about any recent grants awarded for which you have not received the money. Are they reflected as a receivable as required by accounting principles? (Only required if using the accrual basis of accounting).

- Do you carry any **inventory**? Books or tee-shirts? Now is the time to do a physical inventory and verify that the number of items you actually have ties to the value on your balance sheet.

- **Prepaid expenses** often need to be investigated. Tie the balance of prepaid postage to the postage meter. Did part of the insurance bill get coded to prepaid last year? Is it time to record the expense? Look at anything in the prepaid accounts and determine if they should stay on the balance sheet or be moved to the statement of activities (income statement).

- Do you have a list of **furniture and equipment**? Does it match the value on your balance sheet? Even if your accountant records depreciation for you, it is a good idea to walk around and see if the assets are still there. Notate any that have been lost or sold. Add any new computers or other assets that are not on the list (if they are above your capitalization level). If the total dollars on your list do not equal your balance sheet account, some items may have been recorded to the expenses.

- Print out the **accounts payable** aging. The payable aging shows which bills are owed and how old they are. Are bills incurred in the last fiscal year missing? If so, you may need to record those charges. Are your credit cards current? If you have charges since the last statement, you may need to accrue these in an **accrued liability** account.

- **Payroll tax liabilities** should tie to your payroll reports. Any other **accrued liabilities** should be documented.

After making any corrections/adjustments, reprint your balance sheet and place all of the documentation you have compiled behind it. If you put it in the order they are listed on the balance sheet, your auditor will be impressed with your organization.

In planning for your audit, I'd recommend you gather, print, or have in an electronic file the following information as of the last day of the period being audited:

- Board Minutes
- Contracts, including employment, rent, insurance, etc.
- Payroll reports from the outside service or detail files
- Copies of the year-end donor acknowledgements
- Copies of 1099s and the 1096
- Copies of W-2s and the W-3

Additionally, you will need to review your internal accounting controls and policies with the auditors. Reread the first chapter and document your procedures. Once you have all this data gathered, the audit should go very smoothly.

H.   Summary

At year end, you will need to send employees W-2s and vendors 1099s. These are also sent with a transmittal W-3 and 1096, respectively, to the government. Quarterly or annual tax deposits and filings are also required. Your donors expect a donor acknowledgement in January, and you have an idea of what to pull together for your audit committee.

> *Wow! You now know how to record your transactions, produce financial reports, and survive an audit. In the final chapter, we'll discuss important items to consider if you are establishing a new church.*

XVI.   Administrative Issues

Hopefully, you are feeling more comfortable with the accounting requirements of a church. But there are always administrative items you may need to think about. In this chapter, we'll go over:

- The basic steps needed to start a church.
- How to organize the church office.
- Recommendations for a record retention policy.

A.   Basic Steps to Start a New Church

If you are interested in starting a new church, there are some basic steps you will need to follow. Do NOT consider this legal advice as every state and locality is different. You will need to find a local attorney with knowledge of the requirements for your specific location.

Starting points for a new church include:

1. Pick a name. This seems basic, but you can't fill out any of the necessary forms without a name.

2. Have an address. A post office box may make sense if you will be using temporary quarters or haven't yet found a location. PO boxes are inexpensive and will save you time later changing stationary and change of address forms if you don't have a permanent location.

3. Find out the rules for incorporating in your state. This is where an experienced nonprofit attorney will be invaluable. To be incorporated as a nonprofit, there is specific wording necessary in the by-laws, a board of directors may be needed, and there may be annual filing requirements. Inquire as to the risk to your members individually if the church is not incorporated.

4. Develop by-laws even if they are not required in your state. In the next section, we'll discuss the guidelines for writing church by-laws.

5. Apply for a Federal Employer Identification Number (EIN). This is the EIN we discussed in the chapters on payroll. It is required for payroll filings, and most banks now require it before you can open an account.

6. Apply for a State Identification Number, if applicable. Some states simply use the Federal EIN, but others have their own IDs.

7. Once you have the EIN, you should open a church checking account. It is CRUCIAL to keep the church's funds separate from any personal funds. Most banks waive the service charges for churches and other nonprofits. If your bank charges a monthly fee, shop around to other banks.

8. Request a sales tax exemption from your state. This can save a church a substantial amount of money. Be sure to understand and follow the rules of when you can use the exemption. Instead of exempting nonprofit organizations, some states refund the sales tax after it has been paid. Either way, you will need to request exempt status from your state agency.

9. Determine if the minister should be treated as an employee or independent contractor. Document the minister compensation package as discussed in Chapter XII.

10. Determine who will take care of the financial information and how it will be handled. Remember, the person handling the money should not have access to the records.

Obviously, there are many non-legal or administrative steps needed to get the church started like prayerful guidance, building a congregation, finding a meeting space. But be sure you have completed all of the necessary state, local, and federal requirements so you can focus on the spiritual.

B.   Church By-Laws

By-laws are used to define the guidelines and procedures to operate your church. They can be very detailed or more general.

> *Please NOTE: Each state has a non-profit corporation statute that may require the by-laws to be modified to meet that state's requirements.*

Terressa Pierce of www.freechurchforms.com has the following guidelines to writing church by-laws:

1. Meet with the church board to decide your by-laws and determine the focus of your church. The secretary of the board should take minutes for the bylaw meeting.

2. Include the church's official name, bank documents, bills, bank accounts, and other pertinent documentation.

3. Define the church's purpose, what you plan to address through your ministries, and your legal status. Is your church a registered tax-exempt non-profit organization, or do you have another tax status? This will help define how you will operate in terms of donations as only non-profit organizations can accept tax-deductible donations.

4. Discuss the denomination of your church. If your church belongs to a specific denomination, it's important that you mention this in your by-laws. This will help guide your church's statement of faith or what your congregation holds to be true.

5. Develop your church's mission statement and outline how the leaders of your church plan to achieve its purpose and goals. Will your church focus on outreach projects or programs?

6. Discuss the requirements for membership in your church, including the process of becoming a member and each congregant's rights, and responsibilities. Include whether congregants will have voting rights or if the voting rights are held solely by the board.

7. Define how board members are chosen or elected and their responsibilities within the congregation. Clearly outline how the choosing or election process will work.

8. Include the rules for board meetings, including who has the right to vote, how the meetings will be regulated, and how often financial updates should occur.

9. Define the departments within your church, such as finance, women's ministry, youth ministry, pro-life or other areas that your church will focus on.

10. Discuss the church's ability to own land and have assets and whose name they will be listed under. A church must abide by state laws. Some states require incorporation in order to own land.

11. Explain how your church's by-laws can be amended and if majority vote is required. As the church grows, revisions may need to be made.

12. Plan in case the church might be dissolved and how church assets will be distributed if the church closes.

13. Hold a vote to approve the by-laws. If a majority of the board members approve it, this will be a legally-binding document to guide the church.

Terressa's sample of church by-laws can be found on her website, www.freechurchforms.com.

Freechurchforms.com is one of the best resources on the web for churches. It was founded by Terressa Pierce, a women with over 30 years of administrative experience who loves to develop forms. And I, for one, truly appreciate her gift. Terressa has developed hundreds of forms for churches for almost every conceivable event. She also has a complimentary monthly newsletter with great advice.

C. Organize the Office

Whether you are in an established church office or working out of your car, an organized system of paperwork will give you the data as efficiently as possible. Using Terressa's vast experience again, I am reprinting (with her permission) an article from freechurchforms.com.

Setting up an organized file system takes a little time at first, but you will save enormous amounts of time in the future after it's done.

- *1. Plan & Prepare—If your filing system isn't working for you, then it is time to plan and create a truly effective system to get yourself organized. Putting labels on your folders are good, but this alone will not work. You need to plan and set up a filing system that can accommodate any type of paper for home or office. All you really need for supplies are several colors of 2/5 cut tab folders, some hanging folders, and file labels.*

- *2. Create Broad File Categories—Start sorting your documents into broad categories from your current file system or from that pile of papers on your desk that you have been meaning to file for months. Example: "Church Fundraising" or "Vacation Bible School" and more. These are broad categories because there are many fundraisers such as building, construction, missions, youth camp, etc. At this point, do not focus on details of your filing system because right now it doesn't matter what kind of fundraiser it is. We will worry about details later on.*

- *3. **Subcategorize**—After you have all your broad file categories (documents) in piles, pick one of them and sort through it again, but this time break your paper down into smaller subcategories. Example: "Church Fundraising" could be divided into "Building," "Missions," etc. Be as specific as possible. Don't create a category such as "Utilities" but specify which company (East Central Electric) they belong to and break each one down into a separate pile by themselves. We want everyone to get his or her own separate folder. This definitely will make it easier and much quicker to find the file you need.*

- *4. **Color Code Each Major Category**—Assign each major or broad category of paperwork a different color, whichever you prefer, and then put each subcategory into that color of file folder. After you get through with the folders, then all of that major category folders will go into one file hanging folder if possible. Example: "Church Fundraising" might be yellow, and each of your fundraising accounts (Building, Missions, Youth Camp) will have a separate yellow file folder. This might seem strange, but color-coding your file system will save you lots of your precious time in filing and retrieving your papers. Just imagine looking into your filing system and seeing all your folders filled with paperwork broken down by color. They are stacked neatly in hanging folders, and, because you know what color your "Church Fundraising" file is, you find your hand naturally reaching for the correct part of your file drawer. Now that's organization!*

- *5. **Creating Labels**—Once you have the files color coded, label each subcategory. Label one hanging folder per each major category stating the name (Church Fundraising, Vacation Bible School, etc.). I personally like labels you can see from the front, top, or back of the folder. You can also print them from your computer, which makes them easier to read and will help with organization. Do not create a label called "Visa" for your subcategory folder credit card, because if you have more than one credit card they will be separated. Keep them together by creating labels called "Credit Card: Visa." Now when you create more folders for credit cards, they will be all together.*

  FYI: Remember to keep related files in close proximity with each other and do this with every grouping of files until you have labeled every file in each major category.

- ***6. Filing Documents into Your Filing Drawer**—This is your last step! All you have to do now is put your files within each major category in alphabetical order in hanging folders, placing as many folders as you can in each hanging folder without overcrowding. Make your color folders line up as straight as possible in the drawer for easy reading.*

When the time comes to find a document or to put something in a folder, look first for the correct major category by color and then by label.

With an organized file system, it is easy to put your hands on the correct file without a lot of searching. I hope you find this filing system to be as easy for you as it is for me. I love it!

As you can see, Terressa is passionate about her mission. Check out her site for other great administrative and organizing tips.

D.   Record Retention

Once the year is closed out and all the quarterly and annual filings are completed, it is time to review your record retention policy. The basic IRS rules are to keep most records three years and all employment tax records at least four years after the date the tax is paid. If the IRS finds fraud, they can go back seven years for an audit. In order to play it safe, keep your financial records for seven years.

1.   Records to keep forever

There are a few things that should be kept as long as the church is functioning. These include:

- Incorporation papers
- By-laws
- Titles to property
- Any legal documents
- Vital records (baptisms, weddings, etc.)
- Permanent restricted funds documents
- Retirement and pension records.

If you think it is really important, save it. They should be kept in a fire-proof safe or safety deposit box.

2.   Records to keep for an extended period

Some documents need to be retained for an extended period as they pertain to long-term assets. Property records, i.e. mortgage documents, and equipment and other property purchase records should be kept for at least three years after you dispose of the property or pay off the loans. Check with your bank or insurer as they may have other guidelines.

3.   Records to keep for 7 years

Any financial information the IRS may require during an audit should be kept 7 years. Only three years is required, but if fraud is discovered, the IRS can go back seven years, so be prepared. As a whole, IRS agents are trained to differentiate fraud from "stupid" mistakes. But as you may not know if someone in your organization is committing fraud, it is a good idea to keep the financial data for the full seven years and includes invoices, bank statements, cancelled checks or scans of the checks, employee reimbursements, and audit reports.

Employment records should be kept for at least 7 years after the employee leaves and MUST be kept in a locked, secure location. Your employment files should include:

- Applications for employment
- W-4 forms for each employee
- Personnel files
- Performance appraisal and evaluation forms
- Employee handbook
- Immigration I-9 form

Electronic information needs to be backed up and protected. If you have elected to have your bills and banks statements sent electronically, you do not have to print them out to save them. But you do have to assure you can access them and that there is adequate backup. I recommend backing up the financial system and all electronic statements to a flash drive after the end of each year. Clearly mark the flash drive with the contents and store in a fire-proof safe or safety deposit box for at least three years.

Do NOT store the backup files on the same computer as the original documents. Computers crash, get upgraded, or sometimes, simply disappear.

4. Keep the historical data organized

It doesn't do any good to have saved all the necessary information if you can't find it. Carefully label each box with the contents and mark a **Destroy By** date on it. Within the boxes, have the contents well labeled and filed alphabetically or in some rational fashion.

E. In Conclusion

I hope the information in this book will help your church take care of the financial and administrative nuts and bolts so you can better focus on your spiritual mission.

It has been my privilege and pleasure to be The Accountant Beside You on this journey through the crucial overviews and important details of church accounting. I have thoroughly enjoyed connecting with my readers on my website and have learned so much from their stories and questions. Please come visit me at www.accountantbesideyou.com. There are videos and blog posts covering various accounting issues as well as suggestions and comments from others.

XVII.   Appendix

A. **Example Chart of Accounts**

Account	Type	Description
1100 · Cash and Marketable Securities	Bank	
1110 · Checking Account	Bank	Rename with your bank name
1120 · Investment Accounts	Bank	Rename with your investment account name
1190 · Petty Cash	Bank	For cash or gift cards held at the church
1300 · Accounts Receivable	Accounts Receivable	Unpaid or unapplied customer invoices and credits
1310 · Pledges Receivable	Accounts Receivable	Unpaid pledges by members
1320 · Accounts Receivable	Accounts Receivable	Monies due from others.
1330 · Sales Tax Receivable	Accounts Receivable	Only necessary if your state reimburses sales taxes paid
1200 · *Undeposited Funds	Other Current Asset	Funds received but not yet deposited to a bank account
1210 · Inventory Asset	Other Current Asset	Costs of inventory purchased for resale
1400 · Prepaid Assets	Other Current Asset	
1410 · Prepaid Insurance	Other Current Asset	Record the future periods portion of the insurance paid here
1420 · Prepaid Postage	Other Current Asset	Postage Meter Balance
1500 · Property, Building, and Equip	Fixed Asset	

Account	Type	Description
1510 · Land	Fixed Asset	Land owned by the church (put address or plot number here)
1520 · Building	Fixed Asset	Put address here
1530 · Computers	Fixed Asset	
1540 · Furniture and Equipment	Fixed Asset	Furniture and equipment with useful life exceeding one year
1550 · Vehicle	Fixed Asset	
1580 · Accumulated Depreciation	Fixed Asset	Only needed if you record depreciation
1900 · Other Assets	Other Asset	
1910 · Other Assets-Suspense Account	Other Asset	Use this if you aren't sure which asset account to post to
2100 · Accounts Payable	Accounts Payable	Money owed to others
2150 · Credit Card	Credit Card	Add a subaccount for each credit card
2200 · Unearned Revenue/Prepaid Pledge	Other Current Liability	
2210 · Unearned Revenue/Prepaid Pledge	Other Current Liability	Record pledges received before the pledge period here
2300 · Accrued Liabilities	Other Current Liability	
2400 · Payroll Liabilities	Other Current Liability	Unpaid payroll liabilities. Amounts withheld or accrued, but not yet paid
2410 · Wages Payable	Other Current Liability	Only needed if not using an outside service
2900 · Mortgage Payable	Long Term Liability	

Account	Type	Description
3000 Opening Balance Net Assets	Equity	System account. Should be $0
3100 · Unrestricted Net Assets	Equity	General Fund
3200 · Temp. Restricted Net Assets	Equity	Fund balances of temporarily restricted funds
3300 · Perm. Restricted Net Assets	Equity	Endowments and other permanently restricted funds
4100 · Pledges/Offerings	Income	Normal donations
4110 · Plate Income	Income	Cash from the plate not designated to a member
4120 · Pledges Income	Income	Pledge commitments
4130 · Unpledged Support	Income	Money received from a member not pledged
4140 · EFT Offerings	Income	Electronic Funds Transfers of Donations
4150 · Special Collections-Operating	Income	Use for special collections for church operations
4200 · Fundraising Income	Income	Design a subaccount for each significant fundraiser
4210 · Fundraising Event 1	Income	Use to track income from an annual fundraiser
4211 · Event 1 Revenues	Income	
4215 · Event 1 Expenses	Income	

Account	Type	Description
4300 · Other Operating Income	Income	Money or goods received for services offered by the church
4310 · Donation, Gift, Bequest Income	Income	
4320 · Wedding, Funeral, & Memorials	Income	
4330 · Flowers	Income	
4380 · In-Kind Contribution	Income	Receipt of goods or services instead of money
4390 · Other Miscellaneous Income	Income	
4400 · Income - Other Operating Areas	Income	
4420 · Books/Pamphlets Sales	Income	
4430 Cemetery Plots	Income	
4490 · Other Income-Other Operating	Income	
4500 · Investment Income	Income	Record interest, dividend and investment gains and losses in the subaccounts
4510 · Interest Income	Income	Interest from money market or bank accounts
4520 · Realized Gain/Loss - Investment	Income	Money made or lost from dividends or actual sales of stock. From your brokerage account statements

Account	Type	Description
4530 · Unrealized Gain/Loss-Investment	Income	Change in the market prices. Data is on your brokerage statements
4800 · Net Assets Released	Income	Accountant use only. Used to reclassify dollars that are no longer restricted
5999 · Cost of Goods Sold	Cost of Goods Sold	Costs of items purchased and then sold to customers
6000 · Facilities-Utilities	Expense	Water, electricity, garbage, and other basic utilities expenses
6100 · Facilities-Other	Expense	
6105 · Rent Expense	Expense	Facility rental expense
6110 · Church Building Repairs & Main	Expense	
6120 · Grounds Maintenance	Expense	
6130 · Custodial Supplies	Expense	
6140 · Insurance	Expense	Includes all insurances except payroll related
6150 · Building and Property Security	Expense	Building and property security monitoring expenses
6160 · Pastor Housing Expense	Expense	
6161 · Pastor Housing Repairs & Main	Expense	
6190 · Miscellaneous Facilities	Expense	

Account	Type	Description
6300 · Administrative Expenses	Expense	
6310 · Office Supplies	Expense	Office supplies expense
6320 · Postage and Delivery	Expense	Postage, and delivery services
6330 · Telephone Expense	Expense	Telephone and long distance charges, faxing, and other fees
6340 · Printing and Reproduction	Expense	Printing, copies, and other reproduction expenses
6350 · Software and Technology	Expense	Software, website, and computer support
6360 · Advertising and Promotions	Expense	
6370 · Conventions and Conferences	Expense	Costs for attending conferences and meetings
6372 Dues and Subscriptions	Expense	Membership in service, professional organizations
6380 · Financial Fees	Expense	Charges for financial services-payroll processing, credit card discounts, etc.
6381 · Bank Service Charges	Expense	Bank account service fees, bad check charges, and other bank fees
6382 · Professional Fees	Expense	Payments to accounting professionals and attorneys for accounting or legal services
6390 · Miscellaneous Administrative	Expense	
6400 Payroll Expenses	Expense	Payroll expenses

Account	Type	Description
6560 · Other Payroll Tax Expense	Expense	
6600 · Program Expenses	Expense	Use for miscellaneous expenses that do not fall into other categories
6610 · Worship Program Expense	Expense	Use only if the expense doesn't fall in another account
6620 · Youth Program Expenses	Expense	Use only if the expense doesn't fall in another account
6630 · Adult Education Program	Expense	Use only if doesn't fall in another account
6690 · Other Program Expense	Expense	Use only if the expense doesn't fall in another account
6700 · National Church Allocation Exp.	Expense	For charges, dues, etc. owed to a supervising organization
6800 · Donated Goods and Services	Expense	Offset account for the receipt of goods or services instead of money
6900 · Reserve transfer payment	Expense	Record payment of transfer to reserves here
5000 Other Income-Non-Operating	Other Income	Income received not from normal operations of the church
5020 · Capital Campaign	Other Income	
5030 · Endowment Donations	Other Income	
5040 · Specific Bequests	Other Income	
5080 · Sale of Fixed Assets	Other Income	
5090 · Misc. Other Inc.-Non-Operating	Other Income	

Account	Type	Description
5010 · Specific Gifts Restr. -Non-Oper	Other Income	Specific gifts received for designated non-operating purposes
5100 · Special Collections Pass Thru	Other Income	Use this account to record donations received for other charitable organizations
5800 · Reserve Transfer Deposit	Other Income	Deposit of reserve dollars
7100 · Payments of Donations to Others	Other Expense	Pay pass-through donations to other organizations
7200 · Extraordinary Repairs	Other Expense	For large repairs outside the normal operations
7300 · Capital Expenditures	Other Expense	
7400 · Capital Campaign Expenses	Other Expense	
7500 · Grant Expense	Other Expense	Only for unusual expenses specifically required by a grant
7600 · Interest Expense	Other Expense	Interest payments on loans, credit card balances, or other debt
7700 · Depreciation Expense	Other Expense	Depreciation on fixed assets
8000 · Ask My Accountant	Other Expense	Transactions to be discussed with accountant

B.   Month-End Checklist

Duties	Person Responsible	Completed
Enter all bills		
Enter any vendor credits		
Pay all bills		
Enter any manual checks		
Enter all online banking payments		
Enter all bank drafts		
Enter payroll		
Pay any payroll liabilities		
Enter any invoices required		
Enter all donations		
Enter any other receipts		
Record postage expense		
Enter credit card charges		
Reconcile credit card bill		
Reconcile bank account to statement		
Review Receivable Aging Report		
Review Payable Aging Report		
Review Statement of Financial Position (Balance Sheet)		
Review Statement of Activities by Class (Income Statement)		
Review Income Statement Comparison to Budget		

C.   IRS Website Addresses

Below are the website addresses for the various forms, publications, and information mentioned throughout the book. I've put this list at accountantbesideyou.com/irs-links with active links for your convenience.

Internal Revenue Service Home Page	http://www.irs.gov/
Online Ordering for Information & Employer Returns	http://www.irs.gov/Businesses/Online-Ordering-for-Information-Returns-and-Employer-Returns
Per Diem Rates by Location	http://www.gsa.gov/portal/content/104877
2014 Standard Mileage Rates	http://www.irs.gov/2014-Standard-Mileage-Rates-for-Business,-Medical-and-Moving-Announced
Publication 1771-Charitable Contributions Disclosure Requirements	http://www.irs.gov/pub/irs-pdf/p1771.pdf
Publication 3833-Disaster Relief	http://www.irs.gov/pub/irs-pdf/p3833.pdf
Quid Pro Quo Contributions	http://www.irs.gov/Charities-&-Non-Profits/Charitable-Organizations/Charitable-Contributions-Quid-Pro-Quo-Contributions
Substantiating Noncash Contributions	http://www.irs.gov/Charities-&-Non-Profits/Charitable-Organizations/Charitable-Organizations-Substantiating-Noncash-Contributions
Form 8282 Donee Information Return- Required if received donated property over $500 and within 3 years sells, exchanges, or disposes of the property.	http://www.irs.gov/pub/irs-pdf/f8282.pdf
Form 8283 Non Cash Contribution-statement donor files, but is signed by donee.	http://www.irs.gov/pub/irs-pdf/f8283.pdf
Publication 561 Determining the Value of Donated Property	http://www.irs.gov/pub/irs-pdf/f8283.pdf

Form 1098 C-Contributions of Vehicles	http://www.irs.gov/uac/Form-1098-C,-Contributions-of-Motor-Vehicles,-Boats,-and-Airplanes-1
Publication 4303 A Donor's Guide to Vehicle Donations	http://www.irs.gov/pub/irs-pdf/p4303.pdf
Publication 4302 A Charity's Guide to Vehicle Donations	http://www.irs.gov/pub/irs-pdf/p4302.pdf
List and links to employment tax forms on the IRS website.	http://www.irs.gov/Businesses/Small-Businesses-&-Self-Employed/Employment-Tax-Forms
SS4 Application for Employer Identification Number	http://www.irs.gov/pub/irs-pdf/fss4.pdf
Form 1099-to report payments to independent contractors.	http://www.irs.gov/pub/irs-pdf/i1099msc.pdf http://www.irs.gov/pub/irs-pdf/f1099msc.pdf
Form 1096 Annual Transmittal & Summary for 1099 forms	http://www.irs.gov/uac/Form-1096,-Annual-Summary-and-Transmittal-of-U.S.-Information-Returns
W-9 Request for Taxpayer Identification Number Required for independent contractors.	http://www.irs.gov/uac/Form-W-9,-Request-for-Taxpayer-Identification-Number-and-Certification http://www.irs.gov/pub/irs-pdf/fw9.pdf
W-2 , Wage and Tax Statement-Required to be completed for each employee after year end.	http://www.irs.gov/uac/Form-W-2,-Wage-and-Tax-Statement http://www.irs.gov/pub/irs-pdf/iw2w3.pdf
W-3 Transmittal of Wage & Tax Statements	http://www.irs.gov/pub/irs-pdf/fw3.pdf
W-4 Employee Withholding Allowance Certificate-to be completed when hired and changed as needed.	http://www.irs.gov/pub/irs-pdf/fw4.pdf
I-9 Employment Verification Eligibility-used when hiring.	http://www.uscis.gov/sites/default/files/files/form/i-9.pdf
Circular E-Employer's Tax	http://www.irs.gov/publications/p15/index.h

Guide-contains schedules to calculate federal income tax withholding.	tml
Publication 15b- Fringe Benefit Rules	http://www.irs.gov/publications/p15b/ar02.html
Form 941 Quarterly Federal Tax Return	http://www.irs.gov/pub/irs-pdf/f941.pdf
Form 944 Annual Federal Tax Return-only use if the IRS has sent you permission in writing.	http://www.irs.gov/pub/irs-pdf/f944.pdf
Self- Employment Tax Center-Ministers have dual status as employees and self-employed.	http://www.irs.gov/Businesses/Small-Businesses-&-Self-Employed/Self-Employed-Individuals-Tax-Center
SE Self-Employment Tax	http://www.irs.gov/pub/irs-pdf/f1040sse.pdf http://www.irs.gov/pub/irs-pdf/i1040sse.pdf
Form 4361 Exemption from Self-Employment Tax	http://www.irs.gov/uac/Form-4361,-Application-for-Exemption-From-Self-Employment-Tax-for-Use-By-Ministers,-Members-of-Religious-Orders-and-Christian-Science-Practitioners
Form 1040 ES-Estimated Taxes-filed by the minister quarterly.	http://www.irs.gov/pub/irs-pdf/f1040es.pdf

D. List of State Websites

For your convenience, I have included a list of each state's Department of Revenue and Secretary of State (or its equivalent). This list is also available with active links at http://accountantbesideyou.com/state-weblinks/.

State	Department of Revenue	Secretary of State
Alabama	http://www.ador.alabama.gov/	http://www.sos.state.al.us/
Alaska	http://www.revenue.state.ak.us	http://alaska.gov/businessHome.html
Arizona	http://www.azdor.gov/	http://www.azsos.gov/
Arkansas	http://www.dfa.arkansas.gov/	http://www.sos.arkansas.gov
California	http://www.taxes.ca.gov/	http://www.sos.ca.gov/
Colorado	https://www.colorado.gov/revenue	http://www.sos.state.co.us/
Connecticut	http://www.ct.gov/drs/	http://www.ct.gov/sots
Delaware	http://revenue.delaware.gov/	http://sos.delaware.gov/
Florida	http://dor.myflorida.com/dor/	http://dos.myflorida.com/
Georgia	https://etax.dor.ga.gov/	http://sos.ga.gov/
Hawaii	http://tax.hawaii.gov/	https://portal.ehawaii.gov/business/
Idaho	http://tax.idaho.gov/	http://www.sos.idaho.gov/
Illinois	http://www.revenue.state.il.us/	http://www.cyberdriveillinois.com/
Indiana	http://www.in.gov/dor/	https://secure.in.gov/sos
Iowa	https://tax.iowa.gov/	http://sos.iowa.gov/
Kansas	http://ksrevenue.org/	http://www.sos.ks.gov/
Kentucky	http://revenue.ky.gov/	http://www.sos.ky.gov
Louisiana	http://www.rev.state.la.us/	http://www.sos.la.gov
Maine	http://www.state.me.us/revenue/	http://www.maine.gov/sos

State	Department of Revenue	Secretary of State
Maryland	http://taxes.marylandtaxes.com/	http://www.sos.state.md.us/
Massachusetts	http://www.mass.gov/dor/	http://www.sec.state.ma.us/
Michigan	http://michigan.gov/taxes	http://www.michigan.gov/sos
Minnesota	http://www.revenue.state.mn.us/	http://www.sos.state.mn.us
Mississippi	http://www.dor.ms.gov/	http://www.sos.ms.gov
Missouri	http://dor.mo.gov/	http://sos.mo.gov
Montana	http://revenue.mt.gov/	http://sos.mt.gov
Nebraska	http://www.revenue.nebraska.gov/	http://www.sos.ne.gov
Nevada	http://tax.nv.gov/	http://nvsos.gov
New Hampshire	http://www.revenue.nh.gov/	http://sos.nh.gov/
New Jersey	http://www.state.nj.us/treasury/revenue/	http://www.state.nj.us/state/
New Mexico	http://www.tax.newmexico.gov/	http://www.sos.state.nm.us/
New York	http://www.tax.ny.gov/	http://www.dos.ny.gov/
North Carolina	http://www.dor.state.nc.us/	http://www.sosnc.com/
North Dakota	http://www.nd.gov/tax/	http://www.nd.gov/sos/
Ohio	http://www.tax.ohio.gov/	http://www.sos.state.oh.us/SOS/
Oklahoma	http://www.oktax.state.ok.us/	https://www.sos.ok.gov/
Oregon	http://www.oregon.gov/dor/	http://sos.oregon.gov
Pennsylvania	http://www.doreservices.state.pa.us	http://www.portal.state.pa.us/portal/server.pt/community/department_of_state/12405
Rhode Island	http://www.dor.ri.gov/	http://sos.ri.gov/

State	Department of Revenue	Secretary of State
South Carolina	http://www.sctax.org/	http://www.scsos.com/
South Dakota	http://dor.sd.gov/	https://sdsos.gov/
Tennessee	http://www.state.tn.us/revenue/	http://www.tn.gov/sos/
Texas	http://www.window.state.tx.us/taxes/	http://www.sos.state.tx.us/
Utah	http://www.tax.utah.gov/	http://www.corporations.utah.gov/
Vermont	http://www.state.vt.us/tax/	https://www.sec.state.vt.us/
Virginia	http://www.tax.virginia.gov/	https://commonwealth.virginia.gov/
Washington	http://dor.wa.gov/	http://www.sos.wa.gov/
West Virginia	http://www.revenue.wv.gov/	http://www.sos.wv.gov/
Wisconsin	http://www.dor.state.wi.us/	http://www.sos.state.wi.us/
Wyoming	http://revenue.wyo.gov/	http://soswy.state.wy.us/

Index

A

B

C